P

# AN UNAPOLOGETIC SPINSTER

"Never have we read a book about dating that is so real, fascinating, witty, and inspiring all at the same time. But, then again, we've been married since the age of dinosaurs and never read a book about dating before. Regardless, we couldn't have enjoyed our daughter's talented storytelling more . . . unless perhaps she had omitted a few of those dating details a parent doesn't want to know. A must-read for anyone with a pulse!"

**JOHN & SUSAN C., THE PROUD PARENTS**

"Secretly, or not-so-secretly now, I wish my dating story with Christiana had made the pages of this excellent read. She weaves together the subtle details of modern dating to take us on a journey that is relatable, humorous, and even sometimes cringeworthy. In the absence of a *New York Times* book review for *An Unapologetic Spinster*, please accept my rating—An Unapologetic Two Thumbs Up!"

**MIKE F., A FRIEND-ZONED DATE**

"Let's be clear: this is *not* a dating advice book. After all, Christiana has gone on a few hundred first dates over the past five years and she's still a spinster! Whether you're single or attached, we are reminded that we all share similar doubts about our place in society. We are also reminded that we can find love in the most unexpected ways. A brilliant and bold read!"

**MARNIE V., A FELLOW DATING CONFIDANTE**

"I may be a happily married woman but I am not exempt from wondering what is behind the mysterious curtain of today's dating world. This book started as a semi-secret blog of which I was an honored reader. With every new post, I demanded Christiana write more! 'Gimme more,' I said! I like to think I am the reason the blog became this book. So, you're welcome to all the satisfied readers out there! With an exceptional characterization of her nuanced experiences, we go behind that curtain in a way that makes us feel as though we are right there with her, experiencing it ourselves. The balance of humor and seriousness is perfect. Well done, my fabulous spinster friend!"

**ALLIE C., A HAPPILY MARRIED WOMAN**

**MASCOT**
B O O K S

**www.amplifypublishinggroup.com**

*An Unapologetic Spinster: True Modern Dating Stories*

*Chapter sketches by Alexandra Minor*

**For more information, please contact:**
Mascot Books, an imprint of Amplify Publishing Group
620 Herndon Parkway, Suite 320
Herndon, VA 20170
info@amplifypublishing.com

Library of Congress Control Number: 2022911794

CPSIA Code: PRV0922A

ISBN-13: 978-1-63755-328-2

Printed in the United States

## DEDICATED TO MY FUTURE HUSBAND

Look at all the shit I had to go through to find you!
But on the way to you, I found myself.
For that, I am eternally grateful.

The love we all so desperately seek is already within us.

To Nancy -
A fellow author
on a very special journey.
Wishing you all the success,
happiness and health you
dream about.
Much love xoxo
Christabel J

# AN UNAPOLOGETIC SPINSTER

## TRUE MODERN DATING STORIES

Christiana Cioffi

# CONTENTS

# FOREWORD

## BY ALEXANDRA MINOR

Christiana and I first met in our mother's uterus when she and I were zygotes, sharing the same amniotic sac. It was dark and quiet for the most part in our little shared "room." I would even go so far as to say it was pleasant, except for the fact that she occasionally took more than her fair share of the food. Apparently, I was constantly touching her with my cold feet, she has told me. In my defense, it was a cramped space, and she was probably stretching out into my half. Eventually, I decided to kick her with my tiny cold feet, quite literally, out of the womb and into the real world.

I spent the next eight minutes hiding from the doctor and my parents, all of whom were ignorant to the fact that I even existed in that dark, velvety space. It was the early 1980s and supposedly ultrasounds were not the norm, even in New York City.

To this day, whenever asked who is the older twin, Christie

jumps in and responds before I can open my mouth, "I am, by eight minutes. The best eight minutes of my life."

But really, while everyone in the delivery room was oohing and aahing over her, I was enjoying some peace and quiet for the first time. It was truly the best eight minutes of my life.

What does this have to do with *An Unapologetic Spinster*? Nothing really. I just wanted to take this opportunity, since it's been pent up for a few decades. Christie asked me if I would write the foreword, and I took some creative liberties.

In all seriousness, Christie and I have similar personalities and are close. We look alike, are both hot-blooded I-talians, use the same wild hand and arm gestures when telling dramatic stories, both have a slight New York accent, and are passionate and intense. We are complex beings.

We also share a very similar journey through our life experiences, until we don't.

What I mean by that is both of us grew up in the same house in suburban New York City, playing mostly the same sports, having mostly the same friends, and even setting our sights on the same first choice for college.

We both went to West Point and graduated despite only one of us applying ourselves academically while the other asked for study guides (I'm not bitter). I may have been more book smart, but Christie was probably more street smart. Together, we could take over the libraries and a couple urban blocks if we set our minds to it.

After graduating, we were both stationed at Fort Hood, Texas, for a few years while living in the same apartment and then the same house. We both spent two full years in Baghdad before transitioning into the next phases of our professional careers.

It was around that time when we started to have different general life experiences.

If I were to describe Christie in one word, it would be "fearless." That, she most certainly is. From her first army duty station with a Cavalry Squadron surrounded by men, to leading in combat in highly volatile situations, Christie is quite the badass. Coming home with a Bronze Star and a Combat Action Badge, my sister made me and our family proud. First she survived war and then she survived breast cancer a decade later at a relatively young age. But, really it's her mindset that I find so fascinating, even as her twin sister.

Take for example a recent solo trip Christie took to Turks and Caicos. After making friends with strangers on a snorkeling party cruise, the boat docked for a short period some few hundred meters from shore. "Now," announced the captain, "is your chance to test out the diving board located on the second level."

Christie, never shying from living in the moment, was the first person to run up to that diving board. From that high point, while the ocean waves were rocking, Christie did a backflip into the water some thirty feet below. She recounted to me that diving head (or should I say feet) first into the water ignited among her new and fast friends an energy that had the whole boat enjoying every last second of that Caribbean sun.

Maybe it is the hardships she has experienced in life that have helped her become fearless where some would become fearful. I am not sure. What I do know, however, is that it is contagious.

It is inspiring to watch someone you love find strength in what could tear you down to nothing. She is not perfect, she is human.

Yet, here is this remarkable woman, at the ripe age of almost forty, still single. Christie may be unapologetically her. She may have fearlessly recounted her stories here for you to read. But, she is no different than you if you too are single.

For almost five years, Christie has been single and ready to mingle. *An Unapologetic Spinster* is her account of real experiences on her journey to find herself and her future partner in crime.

While her stories are uniquely hers, if you too are single, these stories are also yours. Written on these pages is the journey of someone similar to you who has found a way to continuously grow through setbacks and disappointments. Learning to find the positive, and in many cases, even the humor, especially in dating.

As usually the first person she called after one of these dates, I can attest to the fact that the stories are at least 96 percent truth. She assures me that she has changed the names and identifying details about the innocent (and not so innocent) people described to protect their identities.

What she doesn't change, however, is her brutal honesty about the struggles in her life journey coupled with the crazy world of dating today. If there is anything I can impart on you as you read this book, it is to find the inspiration to appreciate the opportunities that we each have knocking on our doors every day. There is always a way to find gratitude, perhaps the most powerful emotion. We are reminded by her fearless approach to living life that no one is perfect, no life journey is easy, but we can all find a way to grow and be happy if we can only learn to love ourselves unconditionally.

# an

/an,ən/

*determiner*

1. the form of the indefinite article used before words beginning with a vowel sound

# un·a·pol·o·get·ic

/ˌənəˌpäləˈjedik/

*adjective*

1. not acknowledging or expressing regret

# spin·ster

/ˈspin(t)-stər/

*noun*

1. a woman whose occupation is to spin
2. a. archaic: an unmarried woman of gentle family
   b. an unmarried woman and especially one past the common age for marrying
3. a woman who seems unlikely to marry

**Used in a run-on sentence:**

Christiana is an unapologetic spinster, proudly rejecting the societal norms and expectations set for her as an unwed middle-aged woman while instead choosing to live her life, on her own timeline, beating to her own drum, and without the slightest bit of shame for she is an independent, loving, accomplished, intelligent, and wonderful woman by her own right.

*All names have been changed and many identifying personal details have been changed or omitted on the following pages.*

# AN ENDING
# AND A BEGINNING

## FOR A REASON, A SEASON, OR A LIFETIME?
## SOMETIMES IT IS HARD TO TELL.

Are there coincidences? Does the universe make mistakes? Does it have a sense of humor and like to play jokes on us? Are the things that happen to us truly random?

At 4:00 p.m. on a Saturday in February 2017, I found myself wondering about these things. My partner of ten years and I had officially broken up at ten that morning. The dust had not yet settled, not even close. Our relationship had been several years of a breakup in the making. But that morning we had a calm discussion about it. There was no doubt that we had to pull the plug once and for all.

There I was, only six short hours into official singledom after a decade-long relationship, when a text popped up on my phone.

It read, "Hey Christie, it's Jake. Blast from the past! How are you?"

Jake had been my first crush at West Point. We met during basic training for incoming freshmen cadets. I was only seventeen years old and he was just barely eighteen. I remember the exact moment when I realized I had a crush on him. I could tell he liked me too, but he never pursued me.

I never understood why Jake didn't make a move or ask me out during our time at West Point. He always kept our friendship platonic, but I could tell by the way he looked at me that something was there. For whatever reason, I never initiated a move toward him either.

Before graduating, both of us dated a few different people, ultimately finding our own serious relationships.

We went our separate ways after graduation, but I would hear from him every now and then. We would share updates with each other like where we were and what we were doing, then he would disappear.

There I was, sitting on my couch in suburban Boston, hours after my long-term relationship officially ended, calculating how long it had been since I had last heard from Jake. Nine years. I didn't even know that he still had my phone number, yet there was a text from him waiting for a response.

I decided to respond. What did I have to lose? I was now officially single.

Over the next few weeks, while still under the same roof as my ex despite the exit plan we had both agreed to, Jake and I texted quite a bit. In hindsight, I realize it was not the healthiest choice to emotionally jump into something new right away. However, I don't believe in coincidences.

For some reason, Jake, who lived in another part of the country, decided to reach out to me on the exact day that my relationship had ended. For the first time in over fifteen years, both of us were single at the same time. It was as if he had sensed it. It couldn't be a coincidence, right?

If my relationship had not ended that morning, I am not sure if I would have responded to Jake's text. But I did. And so began a new journey.

Over the next several weeks, I learned that Jake was also coming out of a long-term relationship. The reasons were very different than mine, but the circumstances similar.

Jake and I lived in different cities and both had a lot of work travel. It took effort to coordinate, but we figured out that we could meet up back at our old stomping grounds at West Point. It felt like fate was reuniting us at the place we had met seventeen years prior.

At our rendezvous, we absolutely hit it off!

In every possible way, it just felt so right. It was natural. It was easy. It was mutual. We talked about why it had been so silly to not have dated while at West Point. He confirmed what I knew way back when, which is that he had a huge crush on me for a long time. He was convinced that if we had dated then, we would now be married with kids. He said this with such confidence, and I remember smiling.

Intellectually, Jake and I were similar. We had meaningful discussions and were never at a loss for what to share. As an added bonus, our chemistry was out of this world. We were both incredibly attracted to one another, but it was more than that. It was energetic. The intensity of our connection was so thick you could cut it with a knife.

Our reunion was fun, easy, and real.

In the early days of reconnecting with Jake, I felt hopeful. Perhaps I was so eager to move forward in my life that I was grabbing hold of something without seeing the red flags that were popping up. Or, perhaps I was ignoring them to distract myself from the chaos brewing in my house as my ex dragged his feet on finding his own place.

Regardless, I saw for the first time in my adult life that there was potential for *more*. More beyond what I had ever envisioned for myself. What I had believed for so long to be the best I could get was in fact not even close to what was possible.

Maybe I had just been with the wrong person, knowing way down deep that I didn't want to get married or have kids with my ex. Maybe I didn't know what I wanted. Maybe I didn't know who exactly I wanted to be. Life seemed very uncertain, but it also seemed open with possibilities.

Reuniting with Jake had come out of nowhere and it was opening my eyes to a whole different world of possibilities.

Unfortunately, the "honeymoon" phase with Jake did not last long. Soon after our meetup, Jake did a one-eighty. He withdrew. Not just a little, but totally. He was no longer open with me. I could also tell he was not being completely honest.

The first time he pulled away, it broke my heart. I asked myself whether I did something to scare him away or if there was something wrong with me. And even worse, to which I now recognize the answer is no, was the connection with Jake all in my head from the very beginning?

All while this was happening, it was becoming nearly impossible to deal with my ex, who was still living under the same roof as me.

Emotionally, I had completely moved on from my relationship with my ex. It was a surprisingly clean break for me in that respect. It helped that I had a current love interest to occupy my mind. I felt somewhat guilty, but I know I didn't really have anything to feel bad about.

During the painful months after my relationship ended, Jake and I communicated a great deal. Looking back, I can now see that grasping onto Jake was in part a by-product of an unhealthy, codependent, long-term relationship.

I will fast forward two and a half years and summarize that time as it relates to Jake. He was the epitome of a modern-day submarine of the dating world. He would appear out of nowhere, using all those empty words that fill sappy movies, profess that he missed me, wanted to see me, and tell me I was special. Against my better judgment, I would agree to join him in whatever city we managed to meet in, hoping that maybe this would be the time he would become the man I want him to be. Maybe he'd change so we could still make something work.

But it was always the same. Jake would promise to see me, and I would rearrange my schedule prioritizing him. Our time together would be for a fraction of what he promised because he would have a pathetic excuse to have to leave for some other reason. Or he would cancel altogether.

The cancellations were the worst. He sometimes wouldn't even respond to my calls or texts when I would reach out to see where he was. He left me hanging and at his beck and call. I wondered why I kept finding myself in the same situation. Why couldn't he just communicate like a real man rather than like a man-child?

The times when he would be so kind as to give me advance warning that he couldn't meet up, or that he had to leave early, my hot temper would make an appearance. With no shortage of hand and arm gestures sprinkled in with some colorful language, I would tell him exactly what I thought about him and the situation. I would tell him that he treats me like shit, and that I never wanted to see him again. I would say things that I rationally and logically knew to be true, about how I was giving more than I was receiving. I knew I didn't deserve to be treated this way regardless of the intensity of our connection. Wasn't this not too far from what I just spent ten years getting away from?

It seems I had not learned my lesson from the universe, so the universe kept giving me homework. I lacked the strength to once and for all end things with Jake. I had, after all, fallen in love with him soon after we met, finding out years into this that Jake had also fallen in love with me.

Wasn't being in love with someone enough?

Time would prove that it most certainly was not. Over time, I came to realize that having a soulmate doesn't necessarily result in a viable, meaningful, and loving relationship.

I recognized that I needed to make a change. I was looking for someone to make me happy, but maybe I needed to start making myself happy first.

I began to open up to the universe. To explore what was truly in store for me. I dove deep into my heart and soul to figure out what I was supposed to have learned from this relationship and ultimately how I was supposed to grow from it.

In hindsight, I know now that Jake coming into my life at that precise moment was for a greater purpose. I truly believe that he helped me with putting the nail in the coffin regarding my ex, allowing me to once and for all move forward. I may have been clutching onto Jake at the time, but for better or for worse, I was able to move on from a failed relationship.

Though Jake and I were not going to be able to create a committed relationship out of the connection we did have, during our time together he taught me so much about myself. For the first time, I realized what kind of relationship I wanted. Certain aspects of our relationship proved that you can have a strong connection with someone and that you don't have to settle for mediocrity. I also learned that I didn't have to settle for a relationship where I was giving and not getting the same in return.

Over the next two years, I slowly came to peace with Jake's

ongoing disappearing acts. I started to heal my heart and focus on prioritizing myself. I took off the rose-colored glasses I saw Jake through, acknowledging that I truly deserved better.

To my credit, I never stopped dating other people during those early years, despite my strong feelings for Jake. While he took up so much space in my heart, I convinced myself that I would find someone else. Sometimes I would go on dates with a truly hopeful and open mind. Other times I would just be going through the motions.

Slowly, I came to learn even more about myself and what I wanted. I started to appreciate the freedom I had as a single, modern woman and come into my own in so many ways. It was empowering.

Still, it took two and a half years for me to completely fall out of love with Jake. Shortly after I realized I no longer was in love with him and began to feel truly at peace with my singledom, my life took a dramatic turn.

At the ripe age of thirty-six, I was diagnosed with breast cancer. At first, I decided not to tell Jake the news since I had finally put him on the shelf of "Dating What Ifs."

Eventually, however, I decided to share my diagnosis with him. I sent him an email explaining that I was making changes and consciously choosing to release all negativity in my life. That I forgave him for the way he had treated me, even if he couldn't fully acknowledge his actions let alone apologize for them.

I knew that deep down he was a good person, so I told him that I hoped he was able to find within himself what he needed to fix so that he could have all those things he claimed he wanted out of life. I wished him happiness and fulfillment.

After hitting "send," and my words out in the ether on their way to Jake, I felt relief, closure, and peace.

Surprisingly, Jake responded. He showed sincere support for me and what I was going through, which I never expected given how he had treated me.

We agreed to remain platonic friends. During my illness, Jake stepped up.

Where he had once been like a submarine, appearing and disappearing, he texted me every day, asking how I was doing, offering words of encouragement and support. He cared. I, in turn, supported him and some of the changes taking place in his life. It was a mutually beneficial, platonic relationship. I smile when I think back on that time.

Soon after my surgery, I decided to sell my house in the suburbs and move to downtown Boston. Jake was the first person to fly to Boston and visit me. We had a wonderful weekend together and I was so appreciative of him in my life.

Of course, the chemistry between us still existed. I noticed that I didn't have those familiar feelings of attachment anymore, however. I finally recognized what role he served in my life, even if we blurred the lines on occasion.

Then, perhaps predictably, Jake reverted back to his submarine ways. Historically, his disappearing acts would trigger great disappointment and anger from me. Except this time, I realized that I had no expectations. How can you be disappointed if you put little energy into a potential outcome? It ceases to matter.

Our paths crossed a few more times over the next two years. The last time we saw each other was my last weekend in Boston before moving to Virginia. Not surprisingly, we had a wonderful weekend. His visits were strange bookends to a transformative period in my life. It was as if he was helping once again put nails in the coffin as I closed an important chapter of my life.

Jake's communications these days are infrequent at best, but I have come to accept that. I still care about him as a dear friend, one who leaves much on the table in his relationships. I sometimes get sad when I think of the lost potential between us. What if we had dated back when we were seventeen? Would he have been different back then as a more innocent and trusting partner? Would we have gotten married and had kids? Would we be happy in our lives today?

I don't know the answers to any of these questions, but I do know that I'm okay with the path we chose. I don't believe in coincidences, and I don't think he and I were meant to be together. I think we reunited at the exact time we were meant to.

As hard and deeply painful as my connection was at times with Jake, I believe that I soaked up everything I could have possibly learned and all that the universe threw my way over and over for several years. The biggest thing I learned is to trust that with every ending there is also an opportunity for a new beginning.

I am no longer "in love" with Jake, but I still love him, as a friend and a soulmate of sorts.

# THE UNICORN OR THE RIPE AVOCADO?

## ALL SINGLE LADIES ARE IN SEARCH OF THE ELUSIVE UNICORN OR THE ALMOST-RIPE AVOCADO.

R ecently, I searched for a new series to binge watch. I came across *The Unicorn*. It is absolutely hilarious. Seriously. For other spinsters out there, it will have you cracking up on your couch so hard you might drop your pint of ice cream. Check it out.

The premise goes like this (without a spoiler alert): A widowed man, presumably in his forties, is encouraged by his married friends to get back into the dating world. When single women find out his wife passed away, they flock to him like a dog in heat. They seek out this "unicorn," who has his shit together, despite the tragedy of losing his wife. These women are so sick of the pathetic selection of men otherwise available, that they desperately want to lock down the unicorn before he becomes like the rest of the dating population.

I can't speak to the specifics of the story line in this show, but I liken it to a different, yet similar concept about men in their thirties and forties who are found all over dating apps. The avocado comparison.

Men are like avocados. You know, like when you're at Whole Foods, even during COVID, you're going to be very careful in selecting your avocado. You'll first do a visual inspection. Which ones are too green? Too bruised? Too small? Too big? Ahh, there's one that might be just perfect! So you pick it up and give it a little squeeze to see if it's just the right amount of ripeness to make guacamole (or avocado toast).

Before you know it, you've touched pretty much every avocado in the bin. And you've only chosen one. You take that precious avocado home and put it on your counter. You think that maybe in a few days it will be ready for that avocado toast.

Each morning you go to the kitchen counter, pick up that precious avocado, and give it a gentle squeeze. No, not quite ready. Maybe one more day.

Then, one day, you decide to give it a second squeeze. And, OMG, it's ripe! Before it becomes rotten, which could literally happen within the hour, you pull out your bread and overpriced and underused avocado slicer, and get to making some toast! Never mind you had plans to go to the gym, meet a friend for dinner, or take your dog for a walk. LITERALLY EVERYTHING ELSE MUST WAIT. Now is the time for avocado.

THAT, my friends, is what men are like. They are underripe in their thirties and sometimes into their forties—a bin full of man-children who haven't figured out that it's sexy to be in touch with your feelings. No, they have taken all their previous relationship baggage and shoved it into some suitcase in the attic. Maybe they write it up to a rising career or a busy schedule. Or you know what? They just haven't met the right girl. Whatever the case is, they are a lost cause.

Until they aren't. Until they decide they are ready and quickly unpack that suitcase of baggage, throw stuff in the wash or in the trash. Then they step outside into the sunlight and look around to see who happens to be standing nearby ready to make some toast.

That, ladies, is how the bimbo down the street ended up with the man of your dreams. It's not a numbers game like everyone says. It's a timing game. I don't know when my time will come, so in the meantime, I'm walking around with my avocado slicer at the ready in my fanny pack.

# MY ONE DEALBREAKER

## WE ALL HAVE AT LEAST ONE DEALBREAKER. HERE'S HOW I FIGURED OUT MINE.

Soon after I started dating, I learned that I have one very firm dealbreaker. It's a criterion I've used to evaluate the long-term potential of all my dates since.

Before I divulge what that one dealbreaker is, I will rewind and tell you how I figured it all out. Picture me, thirty-four, newly single, and wondering where the heck I should turn for online dating. Since I had been living under a rock for a decade, I only knew about two dating apps. One, in my mind, was clearly not where I would start. It was known for being just a hookup app. I needed to ease into dating through tried and true methods, like the one I saw on commercials! This seemed like a safe approach. Or so I thought.

So, I set up my "safe app" profile and got to swiping. *This is a strange platform*, I thought. Half the profiles don't have faces! How are you even supposed to know what or who you're matching with? Unfortunately for me and my pseudo-photographic memory, I remember one strange dude who wanted to match with me. Let's just say he was wearing a healthy amount of eyeliner, a wizard costume, and was holding a glass ball toward the camera. Under his profile picture it read, "I have your future" or something equally traumatizing.

You're probably thinking, "Well, that's what you get for going on *that* app." And, in hindsight, that would have been a true statement. You're also probably thinking that either wizard costumes, eyeliner, or otherwise bizarre profiles are my dealbreaker in question, but you would be wrong. I mean, I'm not swiping on those profiles, so they don't even make it to the deal to be broken.

I finally had a match! His name was Matt, and he looked fairly cute! He had cats. (Side note: I've since learned that's a warning sign only 60 percent of the time.) Matt made good conversation over text, and actually seemed pretty funny! He even loved fast cars, so we had something in common. All right, I think, let's go meet up in person and pop my dating cherry!

We decided to get together at a bowling alley/bar combo after work for a drink in the suburbs, halfway between where each of us worked.

I arrived at the parking lot of this fine establishment right on time. I was a tad bit nervous but otherwise excited. I was wearing a cute outfit with some nice jeans—you know, just in case we hit it off and wanted to do some bowling, I'd let him check out my ass(ets).

I walked up to the entrance, looking around. Where oh where is Matt? Hmm . . . I don't see him anywhere. But there was a fella approaching me, wearing all-white sneakers (you know, the kind grandma buys from the discount store for grandpa) and extra baggy jeans. He seemed to recognize me. But this couldn't possibly be Matt, could it? I squinted so I could see better. I realized he may interpret my squinting the wrong (or right?) way, and I didn't want to be rude. So, I fixed my face and let the introduction unfold awkwardly.

Yes, this man was my esteemed date for the evening. But it got better. He looked absolutely nothing like his picture. It became clear his profile pics were from several years earlier. I found out in due time that this is to be expected on dating apps, unfortunately. He was at least twenty to thirty pounds heavier and his hairline had significantly receded. Not that there's anything wrong with that, but again, he didn't look like his profile picture. Perhaps I should have turned around and left based on the mere fact that he was misleading potential dates with his online persona, but I wanted to pop that dating cherry.

Deciding to continue with the date, we went inside and grabbed a seat at the bar. We started talking and I immediately realized the worst part about this situation, which was not about his looks at all, but his complete lack of personality, sense of humor, and ability to converse. What happened to the funny guy who was texting me? Had I accidentally lined up a date with someone else and not realized it? Maybe that would explain why none of this was making sense.

Again, perhaps that's when I should have just cut my losses, but I didn't. We decided to order a drink. Well, I should say I ordered a drink. He ordered two and a personal-sized pizza. *Great, this date is going to go on way too long,* I think. I could be home on my couch with my cat, catching up on *The Real Housewives* and instead I'm going to watch a stranger eat and drink painfully slowly while I try to break the repeated awkward silence by dragging conversation out of him. Oh man, this is awful.

It was so awful in fact that, at one point, he bent over to tie his left grandpa sneaker and I took the opportunity to silently, but very expressively, show on my face what I felt inside. I then noticed that the poor bartender was staring at me from ten feet away. Her eyes were huge, she looked concerned, and started walking toward me! *Oh shit,* I think! Now my date, who is still tying his shoe believe it or not, is going to find out that I make faces behind his back. I quickly waved off the bartender and mouthed, "I'm okay." She took a quick look to my left and got it . . . bad date, clearly. And the mini crisis was averted.

Well, during one of the long, awkward silences of this painful hour, I glanced over at my date. And then I thought to myself, *If we were lying in bed and an intruder came in, who would protect us? Would it be me? Would it be him? Would it be my cat?*

I realized, as he took a small sip of his warm beer, that in this hypothetical scenario, it would most certainly be me that would need to protect us, or we would all die.

And that's my dealbreaker folks . . .

PS—I got off the safe app that night and downloaded my way to hookups.

# THE ART OF HIDING MEN

**DO WE EVER TRULY SHED THE FEAR OF BEING JUDGED?
PROBABLY NOT, BUT WE DO OUR BEST TO HIDE WHAT WE CAN.**

This chapter begins with a vignette about my dear friend Jane. She's in her late thirties and owns a home in a suburb of Dallas, Texas. Jane is a successful, independent, intelligent, kind, and beautiful woman. We like to share stories with each other about our dating fiascos, and one of hers draws a parallel to my own troubles.

One common issue we shared was figuring out how to keep neighbors from knowing when you have a male visitor at your home. <WINK WINK> You know what I'm talkin' about! Neighbors can be nosy, and they tend to be even more so when they live vicariously through your singledom because they have no excitement in their lives.

Back to Jane. She was dating a guy who owned a pickup truck. When he started to spend the night, he would park his vehicle in her driveway in that quiet family-oriented neighborhood. One day, soon after he started to stay over, Jane went to her mailbox. A neighbor, who she knew somewhat well, happened to be walking past and said, "I have noticed a pickup truck in your driveway at night. Are you dating someone?"

Jane's jaw dropped to the ground. Should she care if her neighbor knows she had a man over? Maybe she does care, but why? Is this something to be ashamed about? It is a quiet neighborhood filled with kids, but what she does in her own home is her own business, right? Or maybe not? What if this guy was just something casual and next week she has the guy with the Subaru hatchback over? Would that be a cause for alarm with her neighbors? Would they be talking about it at the block party behind her back? <GASP> Does she have a bad reputation with her neighbors because of her dating life? What will the future look like if every time she steps outside to get her mail, she gets the third degree about her male visitors?

Another dear friend of mine, Michelle, lives in the suburbs of Boston and has a pretty exciting dating life. She's in her fifties and is a beautiful, funny, and sassy woman! She makes her men work for it, which often pays off. Michelle also has a very kind neighbor that she considers a friend.

One day, Michelle was getting into her car when her friendly neighbor, sitting on the porch, asked where she was going. Michelle quite proudly responded that she was off for a date! Her neighbor wished her good luck, and off Michelle went!

I'll spare you the details about this date, but let's just say Michelle was hot to trot for her super handsome guy. And, you never know what might happen. On this date, sadly (in my opinion) nothing happened other than a few innocent pecks on the lips. So Michelle returned home late but still before her car turned into a pumpkin.

The next day, as Michelle took her trash out to the curb, her friendly neighbor called out from the porch, "How was your date last night?" Michelle responded that it was fine. Then, completely unexpectedly, the neighbor said, "I'm so glad you didn't stay over at his house last night."

Let's digest that for a second, shall we? Michelle is in her fifties and her neighbor is concerned as to whether she spends the night at a guy's house that she's dating while she's an available, eligible, single lady? Was it okay if they slept together but she didn't spend the night? Or is the issue that it's inappropriate to have sex before marriage? Why should someone be happy that their friend did NOT get laid? In a man's world, it's the opposite sentiment! Who the heck really knows why the neighbor said that, to be honest.

But this is what I do know. Michelle's very kind neighbor is married and can bang it out every night under the privacy of her own roof and no one will judge her. In fact, people may judge her and her husband if they find out that they AREN'T getting it on regularly! Yet a single woman can't engage in the same act without feeling like her neighbor is keeping tabs on her and making assumptions as to what has happened based on when her car is parked back in her driveway?

Michelle learned her lesson. She now tells her friendly neighbor she's off to go shopping or taking a trip Cape Cod. Better to lie than to get judged, right?

Now, back to me. I inadvertently solved this problem when I had my house in the suburbs, which had a two-car garage. I went through a phase where the guys I was dating and inviting over all drove black Audi sedans. In fact, my ex had driven a black Audi that he obviously parked on one side of the garage. To the untrained eye, there were a few months where it seemed the same black Audi drove in and out of my garage. But to the trained eye, it could be seen that one was an A6 and three were A4s. Not to mention, all had different wheels, with one even having a roof rack! What did I do to limit the time in which a neighbor would have to be able to figure out those differences? I opened the garage door, had them drive right in, and then quickly shut the door so the human behind the wheel was never seen with the naked eye. No, the nakedness happened inside the privacy of my own home with the shades pulled down (usually).

Later, when I moved into an apartment in downtown Boston, there was no sneaking or hiding men. The building had a single entrance with a concierge. There were even a few security cameras strategically placed around. For anonymity, I did what I could with a face mask and avoiding eye contact!

# FOLLOW THE BREADCRUMBS AND YOU'LL FIND CASPER

I'M SURE YOU'VE HEARD OF "GHOSTING," BUT ARE
YOU FAMILIAR WITH "BREADCRUMBING"?

I was super excited about this one guy I met on my preferred dating app one particular month. In addition to being a handsome, educated man with a great sense of humor, we realized over text that we had almost everything in common. We texted for a week or so and had a hard time finding something that we didn't share! Casper Chris, as I later named him, said he wanted to meet up that coming weekend.

As the weekend approached, he never reached out to confirm our upcoming meeting. Thinking he was ghosting me, he reached out at the last minute. This annoyed me and the weekend had passed. Yet, I decided to agree and reschedule for a few days later. When the new date finally arrived, he reached out to say that he was "busy."

I was confused as to what was going on. How do you go from saying you "definitely want to meet up" to completely flaking? And not once, but twice. I was annoyed and disappointed at his almost predictable behavior, which has become all too common in today's dating environment. Previous experience told me to just leave the communication where it was, in the dating app, and move on.

And move on I did. I started chatting up someone even more funny. I liked him! He seemed pretty keen on me too. His name was Mark and all signs indicated he was quite the catch. We moved from the app to actual texting, corresponding a good amount for about ten days. In the meantime, I benched a few people in the app because I was excited about this guy. I have dated long enough to know when there is a sliver of hope in an actual connection before you meet in person. I felt there was potential with this guy Mark.

I'm firmly anti-pen pals, and I usually make that clear in my profile. Mark, however, lived in Connecticut. Given how long I'd been single, dating across state lines was no big deal for me. I have had one too many apps display the dreaded search icon when it's looking for an undue amount of time to find the next batch of potential matches only to come up empty and say, "We're sorry. Try expanding your search filters to find more dates." Hence my dating searches that expanded well beyond Boston into the dating abyss of Connecticut, Rhode Island, New Hampshire, and even Vermont.

With Connecticut Mark, unfortunately, we couldn't get our schedules to coincide. He promised me that he was super excited to meet me and also promised that he would drive to Boston over the next few days to meet up. He said that he would reach out the next day to arrange the time and place.

Tomorrow arrived. No word from Mark.

Then the next day arrived. Still no Mark. I decided to rename him Missing Mark.

I sent him a text. No response.

I know this sounds weird, but it seemed out of character for this guy I never met to just disappear. I started to wonder if something happened to him? Did he get hit by a bus? Did his cat get COVID and he's self-quarantining without access to his phone? Did he break his phone and when he got a new one my number and our dating app connection was gone? Was he completely broken up by the fact that he couldn't get in touch with me? I know that is all ridiculous, but these thoughts actually crossed my mind.

I never found out his last name and his first name was so common. I tried to piece all the bits I knew about him together in order to search for him, only I came up empty handed. No news reports on a forty-one year old from Connecticut who was hit by a bus while trying to text a girl in Boston. How could this be? The only possible explanation, I convinced myself, was that he was obviously dead, and his obituary had not yet posted online!

Two more days passed, and I decided to send him one last text. Pathetic, perhaps. But I was trying to be true to who I was, and I had legitimate concern over this guy's safety. In the text I said that I didn't understand what happened and that I hoped he was okay. And I left it at that.

Then, perhaps because I'm a glutton for punishment, I went through the players I had on the bench and came across Casper Chris still in my app queue. It had been a good two weeks since we had last communicated.

I wrote him a short but sweet message: "How about we meet up? Let me know, I'd hate for this connection to disappear into the black hole of dating almosts."

In turn, he deleted the app and our connection with it. And just like that Casper Chris was gone too.

Goddamn it. What the hell happened? Had there been a full moon or something? Did they sense my desperation? Was I desperate? I didn't really think I was desperate. Maybe, like some women give off sexy pheromones that have the guys flocking to the yard, I gave off a stench of cat fur, oatmeal, and worn yoga pants.

Who the hell knows. I have had this happen a lot over the past few years, but yet I find myself surprised when it happens again. For both these guys, I had actually thought there would be some potential. Back to the drawing board . . . yet again.

The dating world keeps getting more and more weird when we have to come up with all sorts of bizarre terminology to describe the indescribable behaviors of people. The term "ghosting" is so common even my seventy-something parents know what it means. There are so many other terms out there that it's almost a full-time job to keep up.

How do we become aware of these new phrases anyway? Obviously, social media is a hotbed of new vocabulary terms along with TV sitcoms, which are like the *Sesame Street* for today's adults. What better way to introduce a new phrase than through the elaborate dramatization of human behavior in scenarios designed for comedic effect? Except, when you've lived it yourself, you may not find it so funny.

The problem is also that it's not actually a dramatization at all. Sit down with any of your single friends and ask them about their experiences and I would bet good money that they have ALL experienced ALL scenarios at one point!

Zombieing is similar, but different than submarining.

Getting love bombed is similar but different than being ghosted, which is similar but different to being cloaked.

Soft ghosting is pretty much every communication ever with anyone in my opinion.

Benching is a great one for those who have several people of interest in the queue and want to focus on the most promising one.

And the list goes on and on and on. It's as if the more bizarre the behavior, the more urgency there is to create a new term to classify it in order to appropriately capture its nuance. By labeling the behavior, we take what would have otherwise just been a horrible way of treating someone and turn it into a predictable, and therefore almost acceptable, behavior. That sense of normalcy then fuels even more people to act that way when they would never have previously. This is why if we try to explain these terms to our grandparents, they can't understand a word we are saying. We've essentially reinforced a terrible new culture that starts in dating when we give the acts almost humorous names.

I recently learned a new term: breadcrumbing. Essentially, this is when one person gives just a little bit of encouragement to the other during dating. The recipient sees the breadcrumbs and follows them, thinking they are being led on the right path. They also think that the breadcrumbs are legitimate and sincere expressions or acts of interest. This can happen at any stage of dating: before you actually meet, after one date, or after many dates. It's never too early or late to lead someone on! This is what happened to me with Casper Chris and Missing Mark.

If we look at the poor children in the fairy tale "Hansel and Gretel," they are left to fend for themselves in the forest. The trail of breadcrumbs meant to lead them back to safety is eaten by birds. They are stuck in the woods and the story only gets worse from there.

In the dating world, breadcrumbs lead to ghosts. Ghosting is done by Casper. Casper is spineless. Literally, Casper is a ghost and obviously does not have a spine! But figuratively too, Casper is about as pathetic as they come.

Why not just tell someone you are not interested? Maybe you want to bench them for someone else, or maybe you just have no interest. I just don't understand the need to communicate with someone, even if you haven't met, under false pretenses. Isn't it a lot more work to lead someone on than to just tell them you aren't interested, in a kind and respectful way? You know, kind of like what an adult would do? Why is this too much to ask?

The best gif I've ever seen is "The Dating Pool in your 30's" with an image of a neglected swimming pool, a couple of inches of nasty green water on the bottom, a few deflated floaties in the corner, and a broken down lawn chair sitting alone in the deep end.

I realize through my month of Missing Mark and Casper Chris that I'm looking for someone to be truly present in life. I'm not looking for the peripheral significant other who floats around and into your life at their discretion. No thank you, man-children. I'm throwing you back into the dating pool of middle-aged rejects. I may be up-to-date on my tetanus shot, but I'm not looking to get a bad case of diarrhea after accidentally ingesting the nasty water from this dating pool.

You know the old saying: When someone shows you who they are, believe them. Hard pass on the deflated floaties, thank you.

# THE FAMILIAR FACE DILEMMA: NAMASTE EDITION

## WHEN YOUR DATING LIFE GETS IN THE WAY OF REAL LIFE . . . OR MAYBE IT'S THE OTHER WAY AROUND.

For anyone who's been on dating apps for a long enough period of time, the following story is for you.

The universe has a sense of humor and inevitably, you will come across someone you know and will be faced (pun intended!) with the dilemma of which way to swipe. It doesn't matter what city you're in or how long you've lived there. I've had this happen many times, even when I'm just passing through a city! Thank you, Universe, for further complicating an already complicated situation.

This edition of "The Familiar Face Dilemma" started with my desperate attempt to fix a nagging hamstring and adductor issue. Fast forward several paragraphs if you want to skip the part about me talking about running. Sorry, not sorry.

At the time, I had just finished running a ridiculous number of miles and races back-to-back. By any objective means, it was stupid. And, like most stupid decisions, I was going to pay the price. When I attempted to run the Chicago Marathon in October of that year, a mere two weeks after finishing a fifty-mile trail race that took me ten hours and fifty-five minutes to complete believe it or not, I found I was not actually capable of running anymore. Surprise, surprise! Raise your hand if you could have predicted that.

The first few miles of that marathon were awesome. I felt strong and was able to hold a solid pace. But at the six-mile marker, my right leg cramped up. To sum it up, I, literally, dragged my right leg for the next twenty miles to the finish. I had to scratch my remaining three marathons for the year while trying to figure out how to fix myself. The rest of this story takes place while I sought out answers at my beloved home away from home, a luxury sports club.

This gym provides a high-end fitness experience. This is especially true if you go to one that also has a pool (which I must say is a lot nicer than the dating pool in your thirties) and more space than could ever be used. Like most gyms, it's also a great place to check people out, and you rarely get called out for it. In the off chance you do get caught staring at someone, it's easy for a guy to say something like: "No, no, I wasn't looking at YOU. I was checking out my biceps in the mirror and you just happened to be in the way. But, while we're talking, I gotta say those leggings and that matching crop top look great on you."

Anyway, I am not shy about admitting that I one hundred percent check people out at the gym. I believe you'll find the highest concentration of fit and successful people, because, let's be honest, its membership fees ain't cheap. It's a place to see and be seen. Who knows, maybe one day I will meet "The One" at the squat rack.

This particular sports club had a great selection of classes. In my quest to fix my body, I decided that I needed to start with stretching. I'm getting old, obviously, and my body is rejecting the trauma I've been inflicting upon it. Stretching, yoga, and cross-training must be the answer.

I signed up for as many yoga classes as possible. One was a yin yoga class, which, I could be wrong, was designed for geriatrics. Yes, old people who want to sit still and let gravity do the work for them. This was right up my alley! I could nap and stretch at the same time! Yin yoga became my favorite class.

Two instructors taught yin yoga at my gym. The weekend class, taught by Andrew, was the easiest for me to fit into my schedule, so I became a regular.

Keeping up with my habit of checking out people at the gym, this class was no exception. The average age of the mostly female group was roughly sixty-six years old, so the only person I could check out was the instructor, Andrew. If you figured this out on your own, give yourself a pat on the back!

Andrew fit the stereotypical male yoga instructor, which I believe is an oxymoron since most yoga instructors are female. He was slightly above average in height, had an athletic, yet slim build, a soft, soothing voice to coax the class into a meditative state, and a ponytail. Yes, his hair was longer than mine. Oh, and he wore super wide-leg linen pants and an extra comfy-looking shirt, as if he just stepped out of an ashram in Bali. But you know what? I still thought he was attractive, and I didn't think it was because he was the only man in the room within a decade of my age.

Well, the weeks go by and I had officially become a regular. Andrew learned my name, would come over to say hello before class started and I would say goodbye at class end. I even went so far as to ask him, with legitimate interest, his advice on fixing my leg issue. He showed me some poses and, in that gentle voice of his, gave me some general advice on how to fix myself.

I skipped class one week because I went out of town on vacation and when I returned the next week (with a tan), Andrew not only mentioned that I missed class, but also took note of my bronzed skin. *Hmm*, I wonder, *does Andrew think I'm cute? Is he single? What's his story?*

Slowly but surely, it seemed I developed a little bit of a crush on my yin yoga master instructor. In my imagination, I had determined Andrew's backstory and that he did, in fact, have a crush on me, but we both were playing dumb to keep it as professional as possible for the fellow club members. I'm being a bit facetious, obviously, but this is how the spinster's mind works.

One day during the meditative portion of class, when my eyes are supposed to be closed, I sneaked a peek at Andrew at the front of the room.

*Oh shit!* Andrew had caught me looking. I immediately shut my eyes and involuntarily grimaced in some not-so-small microexpression of disgust at getting caught.

Damn it. I was making matters worse. Now I turned red. Like really red. Shit, the secret was out about my crush!

When class ended, I sheepishly put my mat and accessories away and snuck out of the room without making eye contact with him. I think that if I was rude and didn't say goodbye this time he would assume my embarrassment was because I farted and needed some fresh air. Who knows.

Regardless, this didn't stop me from going to his class the next week. Yeah, I may have been pathetic but I was also still desperately single! I eventually convinced myself that he couldn't read my mind and all was good.

Then COVID hit and the gym closed. There went my yin yoga class with my geriatric friends and my handsome instructor. What was a girl to do in quarantine?

Well, this girl kept swiping. I swiped and swiped . . . and then Andrew popped up on my screen.

OMG, it was Andrew! He was single, it turned out! I'm not entirely surprised because I had already written his backstory when I was supposed to be meditating.

I recognized him immediately by his long hair and the same wide-leg linen pants, as well as the fact his name and occupation were in plain sight. Then I started reading his profile. Ahh, interesting fact! Andrew had spent time in India for a few years learning to be a yogi. Again, part of the backstory to explain those linen pants. Man, I was on a roll. I read some other interesting facts. Then, two things dawned on me.

The first is that if I could see his profile, it's only a matter of time before he could see mine.

The second is that I needed to decide what to do: Swipe right, and forever let it be known I have (or had) a minicrush. And potentially make it awkward at yin yoga when the gym opened back up. Or swipe left, and dismiss my minicrush as mere desperation in a room full of Golden Girls.

I decided to do neither. I closed the app.

Later, I got back on. Shit, his profile was still the first one up!

I still didn't know what to do, so I closed the app again.

This happened about five times over the next few days! It was if the app and the universe wanted to poke fun at my dating life. "Ha, ha! If you don't decide which way to swipe, I'm going to torture you for as long as possible!"

Then, another thought occurred to me. While I hadn't swiped left on Andrew, I also hadn't swiped right. And, because of my app settings, I would know if Andrew had swiped right on me. I had paid the extra $21.99 per month to get a preview of the "sure things" in my queue. I noticed that Andrew was not in my queue of interested parties. So, there was the answer. There would be no swiping right as, clearly, he was not into me.

I finally decided to swipe left.

I never went back to Andrew's yin yoga class when the gym reopened, but I suppose the mystery of my secret crush was deflated with the ultimatum forced upon me by the dating app itself. I had my chance and I let it go. Probably for the best, right?

PS—The issue with my leg was scar tissue that need to be broken up, and yoga was never going to help as it turns out. Sixty yoga classes and I have literally nothing to show for it.

# A DOCUMENTED BIGFOOT SIGHTING

BIGFOOT DOES EXIST AND IT TURNS OUT HE
LIVES IN THE WOODS OUTSIDE BOSTON.

One summer, I decided it would be a great idea to run a forty-mile trail race in the middle of the woods. I was fully unprepared for this adventure, but I think that might have been part of the allure.

It was a small race.

There I was, about twenty-one miles into a forty-mile race, moving so slow I think a turtle could pass me, but I was still moving along this looped course, in the middle of the woods, and no one else in sight. I had about three more miles until the next aid station.

OH. MY. GOD.

I think my heart stopped for a second. I thought to myself, *What the hell is running toward me? Am I delirious from dehydration or is that Bigfoot???*

It got closer. I realized it was in fact Bigfoot!

Thankfully, it became obvious as it got closer that it was a human in a Bigfoot costume. I laughed and waved at Bigfoot as it ran past me. I don't know why someone decided to wear a Bigfoot costume, but I thought it was absolutely hilarious.

It occurred to me that this person in a Bigfoot costume, in the summer heat, was running significantly faster than me and I was practically naked in my short-shorts and sports bra. That fact alone was a bit demoralizing. Yet I had no choice but to continue on so I could get to the aid station.

A mile or so later, I came around a bend and saw Bigfoot sitting on a rock on the side of the trail. He was not wearing his head (I recognize that sentence sounds weird, but you get what I'm saying).

Bigfoot didn't hear me stomping through the woods and I startled him. This guy, who about gave me a heart attack ten minutes ago, almost fell off the rock he was sitting on. Karma, bitches.

He quicky grabbed his head, put it on his actual head, and mumbled something about how I wasn't supposed to see him. I found all of this comical, not to mention I welcomed the opportunity to not run for a few minutes. So I decided to chat him up.

Turns out this guy was wearing a Bigfoot costume in order to motivate the other runners. I kindly told him he was more likely to make them shit their pants than run faster. Then he told me that the race organizer asked him to wear the yeti costume as a tribute to the local trail runners club that puts on the race.

A yeti? I tell Bigfoot he was certainly not a yeti. He was brown! A yeti is white! Did he not even know what kind of fictional creature he was trying to impersonate? We got into a discussion about it before it was time for me to start running again.

Bigfoot decided he wanted to run with me to the aid station, obviously in the name of motivation as he claimed.

Bigfoot chose to run behind me for about two miles. Yeah okay. We can pause here for a second. We all know he was running behind me to check me out in my short-shorts, lucky fella.

We made it to the aid station and Bigfoot takes off his head, again, and smiles at me. I could tell he was interested. I found him rather handsome in a boyishly disheveled way. I told him, thanks for the motivation, see you on the flip side, and off I went for another ten-mile loop.

Well, because I'm such a slow trail racer, by the time I looped back around, Bigfoot was nowhere to be seen. When I finally made it to the finish line a couple hours later, he was still nowhere to be seen. *Damn it,* I think. I saw the elusive Bigfoot for a moment in time and now he has returned to the wild.

A day or so later, I decided to stalk Bigfoot. I'll purposely refrain from divulging details here as I don't want to be prosecuted for any unlawful activity, but I pieced together the bits of info he told me about himself while he stared at my ass for two miles.

Somehow, I was able to find him on social media! It turned out his name was Ben, which coincidentally goes well with his new nickname. I sent Bigfoot Ben a private message asking if he learned the difference between Bigfoot and yeti yet. He responded. We moved to text.

Turned out Bigfoot Ben hadn't caught my name during the race and tried to stalk me too. It should have been easy for him since there had been a total of fifteen women who had run the race. But he very inaccurately assumed that I was approximately twenty-five years old and hadn't been able to match the female participants by age with me.

I'll pause here—DAMN STRAIGHT I look like I'm twenty-five

when you're running behind me for two miles. Can I get an Amen?!

Back to the story. Bigfoot Ben and I went out on a few dates. He took me to a vegan taco place in the suburbs, which was absolutely delish. We talked about running, life, and all sorts of stuff we had in common. He had a fun dog that I got to meet. We enjoyed each other's company.

I knew that Bigfoot Ben was not my end-all and be-all, but I enjoyed the companionship. I would call what we were doing as somewhere between hanging out and dating (the difference of which is negligible, unless you're an unavailable man and therefore you never "date"). Regardless, we were having fun and I was learning a lot about the ultramarathons he ran, which inspired me on my own journey.

In early fall we both decided to run a fifty-mile race in the woods around the greater Boston area. We met up at the starting line. He gave me a kiss for good luck. The gun went off and the runners took off in the dark, headlamps and all. Bigfoot Ben was sure to be a top finisher; I was sure to be one of the last.

Halfway through the course, Bigfoot Ben lapped me. That proved how fast he was running and how slow I was moving. As he passed by, he gave my ass a flirty smack and off he went down the trail.

Fast forward several hours. I finished my fourth of five total loops, come through the checkpoint aid station, and who do I see in the tiny gaggle of people? Bigfoot Ben.

This is where it gets interesting. Bigfoot Ben and I had been hanging out/almost dating for several weeks leading up to the race, during which he had smacked my ass. He obviously saw that I was running the race as slow as a turtle. When I saw him near the checkpoint, I, for whatever reason, assumed that he would cheer me on as I run through mile 40. I mean, that's normal to assume, right?

Well, I hate to disappoint you, but that is not what happened. I got plenty of high fives and words of encouragement from complete strangers. They asked how I was feeling, filled up my hydration pack, and said very nice, but mostly untrue, things about how well I was doing.

The entire time that I was the center of attention at this tiny check point, no other runners around, my boy Bigfoot was sitting at a picnic table eight feet away, oblivious that I was even there. How did he not realize it? But he apparently didn't.

Well, I realized quickly what was going on. Bigfoot Ben was chatting up a twenty-five-year-old aid station volunteer. He was completely mesmerized by her. I mean, he was so engrossed in their conversation that I could have taken an orange slice and thrown it at his head, and he wouldn't have blinked.

God, I was pissed. What the fuck, dude? Did you suddenly get amnesia and forget I was on the course? Do you not care? Are you literally deaf and unable to hear the people talking to me or my New York accent responses? I'm kinda hard to NOT hear.

I pulled my shit together, topped off my water pack, and decided he can go fuck himself. Or . . . her. I didn't really care at that point.

I spent the first few miles of that last loop being pissed off about the whole situation. And then I realized something beautiful. I was running a fifty mile race and going to live to talk about it! Hell yeah. I'm pretty awesome if I don't say so myself!

I finished the race before the sun set and, of course, Bigfoot Ben and his girl had left the race. I was not surprised at this point, nor did I expect him to be there waiting for me. I assumed he and his new girl were enjoying a postrace vegan taco or two in town.

When I got to my car and checked my phone, I saw that I had texts from family wondering why I hadn't told them I'd made it out of the woods yet. I responded and let them know that I was alive, just incredibly slow.

A few hours later I got a text from Bigfoot Ben. He wanted to know how I did. I told him I finished, and that I felt great. He told me how he did, which was really well, and I congratulated him. And that's the last I heard of Bigfoot. Whatever we had had run its course . . . quite literally.

It may seem like this story ended on a sour note, but it didn't. I like to think that dating in today's world is so much about perspective. If I hadn't met Bigfoot and learned more about running ultras, I'm not so sure I would have ever tried to run a fifty-mile race.

But I did. I ran it for myself and I'm so proud of that. So, wherever you are Bigfoot Ben, thank you for the motivation! Our "relationship" may have run its course before the race was over, but I thank you!

# COVID-19 IS
# A REAL THING

### POLITICS ASIDE, COVID-19 IS THE NEW "FRESHMAN 15."

Being holed up in an apartment in one of the "hot spot" cities during the early days of COVID was less than appealing to me. I had to get out of Boston.

So I packed up my cat and we headed south. My parents live in Virginia, only a few miles away from my sister, and I suppose I could have moved into their basement. But I'm not a millennial, so that was clearly not what I chose to do. I decided to spend the better part of that time living in my sister's basement instead.

I enjoyed my time in Virginia with family. We were a self-contained quarantining group making the most of the situation. Time was flying by.

One night, my sister and I decided to lounge on the couch and stuff our faces with s'mores and watch one of *The Real Housewives*. During a commercial, my sister glanced over at me and said with a great deal of concern, "Um, what do you have going on over there?" as she pointed at my stomach.

I looked down at my pajama pants, which happened to be the same stretchy bottoms I put on two months prior and never bothered to take off except to occasionally shower or do laundry. Uh oh. I noticed a bit of gut sticking out. "I don't know. Maybe too many s'mores?"

She said, "You look pregnant. Are you pregnant?"

I was a bit offended by that comment. Of course I wasn't pregnant. Maybe I had just gained a few pounds. It was probably just a food baby. But then again, other than indulging nightly in too many s'mores, I had been eating nutritious foods . . . I think. I mean, I'd been eating a lot, but it had all been super healthy. We're talking green smoothies, fruit, and veggies. Maybe the occasional pantry raid. But, there was no way I was pregnant.

That is, I didn't think I was pregnant.

Well, I supposed it was possible but also highly unlikely.

Right?

I stood up, lifted my shirt, and we both looked at my stomach. She told me to turn to the side and then said that I looked like her when she was four months pregnant . . . with twins.

Damn it, now I was officially worried.

My sister offered me an almost-expired pregnancy test from the back of her bathroom cabinet. After peeing on it, we waited two minutes for the results.

In the meantime, while hovering over the piss stick, we discussed the possible outcomes. The whole world had shut down so what if it turned out that I was in fact pregnant? Would an abortion be considered an elective procedure? If I wasn't pregnant, I would clearly need to cut back on the s'mores. On the contrary, if I was pregnant, I probably had an excuse to eat more s'mores, or should I say s'more s'mores.

Hearing the commotion from the other room, my brother-in-law came over to see what we were hovering over. Seeing the stick and recognizing a verdict had not yet been released, his eyes got big, and he very slowly backed out of the room without saying a word.

After what seemed like an eternity, the two minutes were up.

The piss stick indicated not pregnant.

Thank God. I was just fat.

# DATING RULES FOR THE SINGLE AND FABULOUS

DATING CATEGORIZATION BASED ON HIGHLY SCIENTIFIC
DATA OR NO DATA AT ALL. HARD TO SAY, REALLY.

**N**ot too long ago, my dear friend Michelle voiced some very familiar dating complaints. She had been on the dating scene for less than a year and couldn't seem to understand why the same things kept happening to her. Guys would come on strong and then disappear. Sometimes they just wanted to talk on the phone and never actually lined up a date. Then there were those that crossed the line from texting to sexting in a blink of an eye. Or the most common suspect—the guy who said he couldn't wait to see her and then was suddenly too busy to even respond to a simple text.

The list of dating complaints goes on and on. And I've experienced them all too. We all have.

I didn't know what to say to my friend Michelle. I loved that she was putting herself out there and going on dates even when it seemed pointless. I was proud of her for being strong and vulnerable at the same time. I hated that she was getting her heart bruised and sometimes broken.

When you tell someone your dating troubles, they always offer advice, some of it really shitty. I've been told to consider lowering my standards. Maybe a 7 or an 8 will suffice? Or to sit outside a fire department in order to pick up a manly fireman. The weird and ridiculous things people say are rarely helpful. You're better off just reading a fortune cookie for advice.

I wasn't sure I had any words of wisdom to share with her, yet I too felt the need to give unsolicited advice. Yes, I had been on a few hundred dates over the past couple of years and literally swiped to the bottom of a major metropolitan area, but I was still single. What makes me an expert in how to do it right? Clearly, I was doing something wrong, right?

Nevertheless, I shared with her some of the lessons I learned the hard way. Here was my advice in the form of rules for dating a man, given that's my area of expertise. A little bit of the blind leading the blind, perhaps?

## DATING RULES FOR THE SINGLE AND FABULOUS

1. If you don't like him, delete his contact info.
2. Get to know him on a date, not over text.

3. Get to know him more on a second, third, and fourth date—NOT OVER TEXT.

4. If a guy wants to see you, he'll make it happen.

5. No sexting. Ever. Don't even joke about it.

6. No sex with someone that you want a relationship with until you are committed or exclusive with said person.

7. A guy who is serious about you will treat you with respect and kindness.

8. If you're not that into him, kick him to the curb . . . unless you just want to get laid . . . and then kick him to the curb.

9. Set boundaries on how you want to be treated. Then stick to them.

10. You don't need to communicate your boundaries and why you have them, but YOU need to act in accordance with those boundaries.

11. Line up a date within five days of matching or move on.

12. Don't ever stop lining up dates with new guys until you are in a committed relationship.

13. If a guy makes you feel bad about yourself, he's an asshole. Kick him to the curb and smile as the garbage truck picks him up!

14. If a guy doesn't call or text when he says he will, kick him to the curb.

15. If a guy cancels a date (doesn't matter why) without rescheduling, kick him to the curb!

16. If his profile pics don't show his full body, Buyer Beware. Men won't swipe right without a full body shot, so why would you?

17. If his profile pics don't have a CLEAR shot of his face, swipe left. A profile filled with grainy pics and sunglasses is as clear as the pictures are not. He's married.

Feeling like I was on a roll, I decided to take the advice one step further, past dating rules, and share with her my strategy for categorizing dates. As a goal-oriented person, I find that these categories have helped me make sense out of how I feel about someone I just met and where I may want things to go. It's all rather simple. I think it makes the most sense to work backward through this process, which is essentially a funnel of men. The largest proportion of dates will end up in Category C, fewer in B, and very few make it in A. I'm sure this categorization can work regardless of the gender of the date, but this is based on my experience in dating men.

## CATEGORIES OF MEN
### Category C: FRIEND ZONE (or No Zone)
### Goal: Friend or nothing

Category C could also have a subcategory called the No Zone, meaning you walk into a bar to meet someone for the first time and consider walking right out before you ever sit down. Or maybe they are pleasant company, but you have no desire to date them or be friends. For simplicity's sake, I'm not building out the No Zone category since you will likely forget their name the second the date ends. Hell, if you're like me, you won't remember their name five minutes in.

However, you need to think about the No Zone because it becomes the exclusionary criteria for who can possibly make it into the Friend Zone. Generally, if you are not attracted to your date, or feel like you "don't click," then you shouldn't date them. However, maybe there's great conversation and you have a lot in common, so perhaps there is room for a platonic relationship. Clearly, the No Zone is for any and all assholes, weirdos, or people who don't respect your boundaries. We ain't got time for that shit.

## Category B: BANGABLE
## Goal: Do the deed

This is a wide category. You may be greatly attracted to them physically, but nothing is there emotionally or intellectually. Perhaps it's
the other way around. You find there's compatibility on an emotional
and intellectual level, but physically it's a big zip. There could be a
decent amount of potential to get along to no potential other than
it being all physical. Any which way you look at it, you're probably
not going to marry the guy.

From my experience, this is the murkiest of places to operate.
You must be very clear about what you're looking for and be honest
with yourself about potential. I have been at this so long that I know
within ten minutes of meeting someone if there's true potential.

It takes practice, but eventually you come to the hard truth that
someone who scores in this category could be fantastic . . . just not
your type of fantastic. There may be nothing wrong with them by
any objective means, but there's something intangible missing in
your connection that makes you think and feel that they are not
"The One." Maybe you don't believe in "The One," but you get my
point. Do you see the potential for a lasting and fulfilling relationship with this person? If "your gut" (a.k.a. your digestive tract),
tells you no, then they are likely in Category B. Like that coworker
you know who will never get promoted, your date has no upward
mobility in your life.

Don't feel bad. I find it's best to be honest sooner rather than later
about how you're feeling, or not feeling, so you don't inadvertently
hurt someone. I have made some great friends, who are wonderful
people, through dating, and while they are perfectly normal and
quite a catch, they are not "The One" for me.

On the lower end of this category are the people you don't have too
much in common with other than physical chemistry. If it weren't for

their pretty face or hot bod, you probably wouldn't want them to be in the Friend Zone either. Shallow, perhaps, but still probably true.

My advice is to date the bangable man, just like the guy who dates the hot girl who has an empty vessel for a brain. Just as the average guy would do without thinking twice, when it's time, you gently place the bangable man out at the curb for garbage day pickup unless you can see a friendship evolving. In which case, be honest and open with them and see what happens. Category B can turn into Category C.

I am a firm believer that you must ALWAYS have at least one trustworthy guy in Category B "at the ready." You must enjoy their company and they must be a good person who treats you well. Category B helps you not get too singularly focused on a Category A person when they eventually enter the picture. Ultimately, however, you need to protect yourself, and have fun doing it, if you decide to date like a man when it comes to this category.

## Category A: SOULMATE
## Goal: Lifelong partner

Look, anyone reading this book who is single likely ain't no young chick. You're aging, and fast. Sorry to break it to you if you weren't already aware. If you are emotionally available, you ultimately want to meet your "soulmate," although I think there are different types of soulmates. I'm talking about "your person."

You know, the one who is going to take you to the ER in the middle of the night if you get food poisoning, hold your hand while taking a stroll through the park, understands you and helps you become a better person, and perhaps for many of us, is the person you hope to build a family and/or life with. They are someone you can truly fall in love with.

This is an awfully tricky category to deal with for a few reasons. First, I believe that there are so few people that will truly feel like soulmates (if you're paying attention to what you're actually feeling). Second, timing can often be off and complicated as we have created our own lives before they enter ours. Third, as we get older, it seems that we all carry around baggage that needs to be unpacked. Fourth, when you do meet, you both might sense the intensity of the connection and move too fast . . . and then everything that hasn't been worked out comes tumbling from the suitcase freaking everyone out.

This is the category where you need to work toward a mutually agreed upon and committed relationship before jumping in bed. That is much easier said than done, especially if you're so excited to have finally met this person. Consciously, take your time and build the emotional connection and trust. And enjoy the journey.

Now, everything I write about above is based on my view of the universe, relationships, and my own experiences. It's not based on any self-help book, and it is probably common sense. However, I think it's hard to remember the common sense part when the dating world is a mess of convoluted games that make you question your own intuition every step of the way.

So, I don't really know if any of my advice is good. I mostly try to follow my own advice yet I'm still single.

Perhaps until I have some proof that these rules and the categorization process are worth a shit, maybe my best advice to you is to not take my advice.

# SLOPPY JOE AND THAT GODDAMN WINDBREAKER

**EASILY ONE OF MY TOP FIVE WORST DATES.**

O ne stormy, Sunday afternoon in Boston, I was stretched out on the couch, still in my pajamas, when I heard the familiar *DING* from one of my dating apps. Sounded like I had a message.

I opened the app to see that my date for later that afternoon cancelled. He didn't sound apologetic either. He wrote something to the effect of, "I had some stuff come up and won't be able to meet up today." I try to treat everyone with kindness and respect, so I simply replied, "Okay, enjoy your day." No need to ask about rescheduling.

Previous last minute date cancellations would lead me to believe it's obvious we're never going to meet.

Rather than feel gloomy like the weather, I decided to challenge myself and see if I could line up a new date for that evening. It was only noon, and the day was still young! I had been on a bit of a dating streak that month and this was my only free night for the entire carefully planned out week. I also wanted to see if I could survive seven straight days of dating.

I started going through my queue in the app. For this particular app I pay extra to see who has already swiped on me. I find it extremely helpful. In general, so much of lining up dates is all in the timing. And with this app, timing is even more important because they can quickly disappear into the dating black hole if you don't seize the opportunity right then and there.

I am proud to say that my app queue is usually pretty solid. Almost every day I sort through it to get the guys that I'm definitely not interested in out of the way. On this Sunday, I scrolled down the queue to check out some of my oldest pending connections.

I saw one guy, Joe. He was forty-two years old and lived in Somerville, Massachusetts. He looked attractive in his photos and rather fit too. He was around six feet tall, had a job, described himself as athletic, and spent time outdoors. What the heck, I'll swipe right and see what happens.

Then I messaged him immediately with what I think was a witty comment. No use in delaying—I was trying to fill up my evening and set a new dating personal record! I continued to swipe on at least five other guys and hoped one of them was bound to strike up a conversation.

Two hours later my phone dinged. I opened the app and saw that Joe had responded to my semifunny opener. Ah, he wrote back something funny too. Great, he had a sense of humor!

The witty banter commenced. Back and forth we went, sporadically, over the next few hours. We started with the weather, moved on to face masks, and closed out with a synopsis of each of our worst first dates. The irony of this last topic would not be lost on me some hours later.

By the time six o'clock rolled around it seemed as if he was not going to pull the trigger to meet up. In an effort to point out that he missed his chance and that I wouldn't be responding anymore that evening, I said that I was off to go get dinner. He proceeded to ask what I planned on having and I said pizza. He then asked where his invite was for the pizza party.

It seemed Joe may want to meet up after all! I told him I didn't have any plans afterward and asked if he would want to grab a drink. He said he was game, and after a little back and forth, it was a plan. We decided to meet in just over an hour at a bar in the South End. This seemed like plenty of time considering it was a Sunday and it would take him all of twenty minutes to drive from Somerville to the South End.

Date time arrived. I decided to wait for him outside the bar during a break in the rain. He was nowhere in sight. I looked left and right, scanning the street to make sure I spotted him before he saw me.

I realized there was a blind spot in my view, so I repositioned myself. Oh, here was a guy walking toward me that sort of looked like Joe's profile pictures. He waved at me. Yup, this was him.

Ugh. As he got closer, I realized he looked nothing like the pictures in his profile. He was at least thirty pounds heavier. Not to sound mean, but he clearly was not the athletic guy he claimed to be in his profile. And . . . what the fuck was he wearing? Was that a windbreaker from 1979? OMG, it is. Are retro windbreakers back in style? And if they are, is that appropriate first date attire?

You know what—it didn't matter. Even if they were back in style, it didn't look good on him. He just looked so . . . sloppy.

I thought to myself, *Oh well, the date has begun so I might as well just keep it moving.* We greeted each other with a smile and hello, pulled up our face masks, and headed inside the bar. As the waitress left us at the high-top and we took our seats, we both noticed on the table a laminated piece of paper with a short message and a QR code.

Now, this was not my first time out and about during COVID. I was familiar with the routine: pick up the laminated (and contaminated) paper, scan the QR code, view the menu, and pay online later. These are the rules put in place and I think they're dumb, but whatever.

Well, Sloppy Joe here had clearly not been out of his Somerville apartment for quite some time. He proceeded to pick up the contaminated laminated paper and read it out loud. Good, he can read. It says something to the effect of, "Please wear your face mask when greeting your server and when getting up from the table."

Sloppy Joe was confused. "So, I need to put my face mask on when our server comes to the table?"

For whatever reason, I became a bit annoyed and I'm not sure why. I said, "No, I don't think it's that strict. That's not something that's actually enforced at any restaurant. It's just when you get up to go to the restroom or leave."

Unfortunately, this wasn't sufficient clarification for Sloppy Joe. Because he had to understand exactly what the instructions were, he got up and went over to the hostess stand. He was well within six feet of her and proceeded to ask for clarification on what to do. I was fairly certain the irony was completely lost on him.

Joe returned back to the table and told me we didn't need to put our face masks on every time the server came to the table unless we wanted to. What do you know! Strike one for Sloppy Joe.

We downloaded the menu, ordered our drinks, and got to chatting. Now, mind you, I already knew that there was no way in hell I was going on a second date with this guy. But, to his credit, he was pretty good at making conversation from the start, which I welcomed.

As the date progressed, he seemed overly energetic. There was something about the manner in which he spoke, and I couldn't quite figure out what it was. There were a lot of strange midsentence pauses, seemingly for dramatic effect, as well as side head-tilting and face scrunching, and saying "like" repeatedly. And his voice . . . there was something about it. It had an inflection at the end of every sentence, as if he was asking a question. Was his voice naturally that high? It hadn't been that high when he was inquiring about the menu, so was he putting on a show for me? Who was his character supposed to be?

Then it hit me. His mannerisms and voice made him sound exactly like a millennial girl.

Yeah, you read that correctly. Now, anyone who knows me is fully aware that I do not consider myself a millennial nor do I particularly care for women who act like the quintessential millennial. I would rather gouge my eyes out than have a conversation with a Lululemon crop top-wearing serial selfie taker who thinks they know everything about life when they literally moved out of their parents' basement last month. Not to mention their voice when they shit-talk about their bestie's latest Instagram post to the other bestie . . . like nails on a chalkboard! No thank you, I'll pass on that.

Damn it, this was going to be a long date. Deep breath. I was there and going to survive it. Among other things, this date was necessary in order to hit my seven date dating streak this week, and I convinced myself it would be worth it.

Sloppy Joe smiled at me and told me that I was very cute. I thanked him for the compliment. Then he said, "Aren't you going to say the same to me?"

Yikes. I hope he hadn't seen the microexpression that flashed across my face. He was absolutely not cute. Thinking quickly, I tried to avoid answering the question and said, "I don't think you're supposed to tell a man that he is cute."

He giggled. Oh my God! Damn it, he giggled AND apparently thought I was funny when being serious. But my response wasn't enough it seems. He coaxed me again for a judgment on his looks. *This guy is insecure*, I thought.

I mustered up my best poker face and told him in a less than enthusiastic voice, with perhaps too much eye contact to compensate for the giant lie coming out of my mouth, that "sure, you are handsome." Note, I didn't use the word "I think" on purpose. He didn't seem to pick up on that. In my mind, if I had 20/40 vision and was a solid fifty meters away, he could have been considered handsome, 1979 windbreaker and all.

He seemed satisfied. Phew. Moving on. He told me his story, which was essentially the same as 88 percent of Bostonians. He was born, raised, educated, and hoping to spend the rest of his life in the same twenty-mile radius of Boston. Definitely not my kinda guy. But we already know this.

Sloppy Joe seemed very interested in what I had to say. He leaned across the table extremely smiley. Perhaps it was the act I sense he was putting on, which I found a bit unsettling. He said, "I think it's really great that you run, and you are clearly in very good shape. Being in shape is so important."

Seriously, dude? Have you taken off that windbreaker recently to see the situation you've got going on underneath? I'm glad you like your dates to be in great shape while you can roll in like that. Thankfully, he didn't take the opportunity to ask me if I also think he was very fit. I didn't think I could handle another lie.

By this point, about ten minutes of the date have passed and it's been moderately painful, but I felt confident I could suffer through the rest of my drink.

For some reason, he asked me flat out if I thought he was my type. Aw, shit. Here we go. I couldn't lie again. I didn't want to be mean, but this was also my out. By answering honestly, I could avoid the end-of-the-date or after-date rejection and respectfully let him down gently.

I kindly tell him that while I was enjoying our conversation (only slightly true, I was mostly just enjoying my drink), I was not feeling a romantic connection.

He looked stunned. I mean truly stunned!! He said with quite a bit of attitude and a much deeper voice, "So you don't think I'm attractive?" Woah, woah, woah. Where was this going? And what the hell happened to the millennial girl? The dude was forty-two years old and it really didn't matter what I thought about his looks, I had been honest that we weren't a match. Take the hit gracefully, man.

I didn't answer him and instead said, "Look, I'm trying to be honest with you. I feel connections or I don't pretty quickly. It's not personal. It's more of an intangible energy thing that has nothing to do with how you look."

It went downhill from there. I believe I've blacked out most of the details, but what I remember is pretty awful. This totally different person, perhaps the real him, became extremely defensive. He accused me of forcing him out on this date and that he hadn't had time to prepare. I had no idea what that meant, so he explained that usually he liked to come prepared for dates with the questions he wanted to ask and topics for discussion. I wondered if he also prepared a different outfit if given more time, but I didn't have the guts to ask.

I told him, case in point, we were not a match for that reason. I was spontaneous and didn't need to prepare for a date. I would gladly meet someone at the grocery store and chat them up if I felt a connection. We were clearly not similar.

That didn't help matters. He went on and on about how I dragged him out of his apartment in this rainstorm and that it was all my fault. He said he didn't need friends; he had everyone in his life except his lifelong partner. He insinuated that I was out on dates under false pretenses. It was awful and I felt attacked, but I stood up for myself and—my parents would be so proud—kept my cool despite his rudeness.

I finally told him he should leave. "Why don't you just go? I'll pay the check, that way you can go salvage the rest of your evening." I waved the server down for the check because I didn't care what this guy's response was. I wanted to get the hell away from him.

Sloppy Joe stood up dramatically before putting his face mask on. *Tsk tsk!* I guess he couldn't remember the clarification he so desperately needed from the hostess a short fifteen minutes before.

Suddenly, the millennial girl was back. He looked at me, about to say something. He tilted his head to the side, scrunched his face up into a fake look of sadness, smacked his lips, and said in an overly sympathetic and truly condescending phony voice that only a millennial girl can pull off, "Best of luck to you."

*Fuck you*, I think. I'm not the crazy person here. So, I channeled my inner millennial girl and I said right back at him, "Best of luck to YOU."

And then Sloppy Joe stormed out of the bar. Good riddance.

Ugh. I felt dirty. The bartender was a few feet away, and when she looked at me, I couldn't resist the urge to vocalize what I just had gone through. I told her that this had been easily one of my top five worst dates with a man-child. That's all I had to say, and I felt better.

She disappeared for a second and then came back with the server and three shots of tequila. We toasted to next Sunday night's date being better than this one, and I felt much better.

Maybe I shouldn't try so hard to set personal records in dating.

It's a marathon, not a sprint . . . whether or not anyone on the date is wearing a windbreaker.

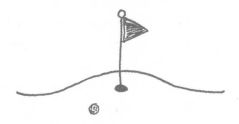

# PRACTICING MY GAME

## IT'S RAINING MEN AT THE GOLF CLUB.
## CAN I GET A HOLE IN ONE?

I have a single male friend in his early forties, who, by all objective means, is handsome, athletic, intelligent, and just a cool dude. He has no problem finding women to date in the real world. Yes, he actually meets women outside the inauthentic technological construct that the rest of us operate in.

This guy has got it going on. He's prime picking for pretty much any woman on the dating scene. All he needs to do is smile and the women start to swoon. And just like that, his Friday night plans are locked in.

I think he's a bit oblivious regarding his own good looks and easy-going nature that allow him to be successful the "old school" way.

Regardless, he likes to give me advice on the best ways to meet people. "Go where the men are hanging out and see what happens," he says.

Where the heck is that? Aren't men pretty much everywhere? But maybe finding them is like how a rain cloud forms. Temperature and climate need to be just right. I decide I need to be a storm chaser and put myself out there like my friend does. Maybe, if the timing is right, lightning will strike.

He suggests I go to a golf course and driving range. There's one just south of Boston that has a great bar, outdoor seating, and view of the city. It's a place to see and be seen.

His suggestion was quite timely, actually. The year before, golf lessons were on my bucket list, but I just couldn't fit them into my schedule. Eventually, I gave up on that idea.

Then COVID hit and working from home gave me more free time. It was much easier to hop in my car after work and get in a lesson any day of the week. I contacted the golf club my friend recommended and signed up for lessons.

I thought that with a few lessons under my belt, I could hit the driving range without embarrassing myself and start picking up men in their natural habitat. Not to mention that I'd be increasing my chances of getting struck by lightning by holding a metal club, at the top of a hill, in the middle of a giant manly storm cloud. I was on the eternal quest to ditch the dating apps.

I took lessons for most of the summer and into the fall. My instructor was awesome: incredibly patient and a good golf instructor. I told him during my first lesson that I want to win "The Most Improved Award." Every week I checked in with him to see if I was in the running to win. At each check-in I was still the front-runner. I believed it also helped that no one else taking lessons knew this award existed, but that's beside the point.

I wasn't terrible at golf. And by golf, I mean just hitting the ball.

Obviously, I hadn't yet hit the links yet. Like running a marathon, I wanted to train and build my skills so that when I did hit the course, I could have an enjoyable experience.

I was so serious about finally checking this bucket list item off that I invested in a solid set of hot pink-and-black golf clubs. I even bought cute golf skorts and shirts to go with my shoes. I played the part and all was going well.

Anyone who's ever tried to play golf knows how technical it is. You must practice the fundamentals regularly. Through my lessons, I learned the basics but couldn't get them all down simultaneously. I call it "whack-a-mole of golfing" because every time I got one move down, I forgot to do another.

I needed to practice at the range between lessons. This was perfect: I was no longer embarrassing or a hazard to others. I could practice both my golf game and my flirt game. Game on.

One warm and sunny weekend afternoon, I decided to go to the driving range. I quickly scanned the open spots and made my way toward the highest concentration of attractive men in my age range. I saw a cute guy and set up shop next to him. I mean, I couldn't actually "see" him since he was wearing a trucker hat and a face mask, but his arms looked great and his swing was pretty smooth. *This guy knows what he's doing*, I think. Maybe I can get some free pointers!

I said hello and hoped he would notice me in my cute little outfit. About five minutes into hitting my balls, I decided to take a water break and glance over at him. He's young, I realized. Maybe mid-twenties? I couldn't be sure. Well, in the outfit I was wearing I could pass for under thirty, so I decided to not let that change the name of the game.

My glance worked. He stopped swinging and asked me if I was from Minnesota. *That's random*, I think. It turns out he noticed the

Minnesota sticker on my water bottle. We get to talking. Perfect. *This is going swimmingly*, I think!

He told me his name was Rick and we chitchatted about some basic get-to-know-you stuff. Thank goodness there wasn't a line to get into the range because there wasn't much golfing taking place at our stations.

Finally, he asked me if I would like some free golf tips, since he's a longtime golfer. Of course I welcomed it.

For thirty minutes or so, Slick Rick gave me tips as if we were in a rom-com. He was definitely not adhering to the social distancing requirements and was getting all up in my space helping me with my grip and swing. I thought to myself, *Who knew golf could be so much fun?*

To be honest, some of his tips were contradictory to my instructor's, but I didn't think he needed to know this. After all, I was finally under a storm cloud with my personal lightning rod.

It was great. I was actually improving just a little bit with his help!

As we were both finishing our buckets of balls I decide it's my chance to close the deal!

I turned to him and said, "Excuse me, [Slick] Rick. But can I buy you a drink for your incredibly helpful tips? It's the least I can do."

Slick Rick smiles and says, "Thank you! But my lessons are free, so no drink is necessary."

WHAT?! I thought we had been hitting it off for the past half hour.

Shit. I realized I was in the bunker. Quick, what club do I need to grab to get out of this thing?

I try again and say, "Really, it was so kind of you. Are you sure I can't thank you with a drink?" I gave him my most endearing puppy dog eyes.

"Oh no, really, it was my pleasure," he says.

Damn it. I was still in the bunker and there was no getting out.

What guy turns down a free drink?

Was it possible this young buck had a girlfriend? Quite possibly. Maybe he shouldn't have been all up in some honey's personal space helping her with her golf swing then. That thought made me feel better. Let's paint him as a cheater in the making!

If I'm being honest though, I think he was actually just a really nice guy. Or, maybe when he was so up close giving me tips, he realized that I was well over a decade older than him. Mental note: line up some Botox ASAP.

As we packed up our gear and headed to the parking lot, Slick Rick tells me that he's at the range often after work. I should come say hi if I see him.

I haven't seen Slick Rick at the range since that day and I haven't stopped chasing other storm clouds if the chance presents itself. Slick Rick may have been a swing and a miss for me, but I'm sure one day lightning will strike. Practice makes perfect, right?

# DOC MCPILOT

## THE ONLY THING HOTTER THAN A MAN IN UNIFORM IS WHEN HE TAKES IT OFF TO PUT ON A PAIR OF SCRUBS.

**M**y experience with Doc McPilot was like an episode of *Grey's Anatomy* colliding with *Top Gun*. Enjoy this one—I know I certainly did.

Man, I know how to date across state lines if I say so myself! Over the past few years, I've flown on the short plane ride between Beantown and DC more times than I can count. My sister and her family live in Virginia, and it makes for a quick getaway.

Within four seconds of wheels down at Reagan International Airport, my dating app flavor of the month would be back on cellular service and my location updated. Without any shame whatsoever, I would let the lucky passenger in 16B take note of my swiping skills as I quickly assessed the local selection. I'd pause briefly to exit the plane and then resume activities at the curb for the predictable twenty-minute wait. By the time my sister finally showed up with her kids strapped in the back, I had several hot ones brewing in the queue.

I became so good at this game, that by 1:00 p.m. that same day, I usually had dates lined up for every night of my long weekend.

One early morning trip in summer 2018 was no exception. I was lucky enough to line up a date with a smokin' hot medical student. He was one year older than me, exactly six feet tall, had a bit of scruff on his handsome face, and was skillful in the witty banter department. He also didn't waste any time and lined up a date soon after we matched.

Our first date took place at a happening bar in Clarendon, across the Potomac from DC. I found it to be a convenient location to meet dates on the regular since my sister could easily drop me off with her kids in the back seat. Giving me the third-degree en route, my adorable niece would ask, "What's a date?" I would respond as only a cool aunt can, "Something desperate adults do when they are in denial about their perpetual state of singledom. Don't worry little ones, it will likely be a complete waste of time and I'll be back soon to go bike riding with you." They would all giggle having no clue what I meant.

On this date with the handsome doctor-to-be, I was very pleasantly surprised that he was even better looking than his pictures. YUMMY. We had a drink or two and shared some vegetarian sushi. Our conversation was easy and enjoyable. It turned out he was also a pilot in the air force reserves. Damn . . . this guy just got hotter! He was also incredibly intelligent, mature, thoughtful, funny, and a gentleman. He was clearly the whole package and then some. I decided to name him Doc McPilot.

When the date came to an end, he asked me if he could see me again that same weekend. I figured I could cancel the other first date I had lined up for the next day and agreed to go out with him again.

The next day, just as it's almost time for him to pick me up, my sister decides to give me the third degree, obviously living vicariously through my freedom. She followed me around the house, holding a dirty diaper in one hand and a look of complete exhaustion on her face. She wanted to know where I was going, what we'd be doing, and when I would be home. I didn't answer her since I knew she would just stalk me on the Friend Finder app anyway. I found out later that she takes screenshots of my location every thirty minutes in case she needs to contact the authorities.

Oh, he's already here! I darted out the door telling my nieces to stay inside. I didn't need them scaring off Doc McPilot.

As I got into the car, I glanced back at the house. OMG! All three of them have pressed their faces against the window and were waving frantically. My sister was laughing. Clearly, she thought it must be fun to embarrass me. But the joke was on her; she was still holding that dirty diaper.

I hoped Doc McPilot wouldn't look at the house and notice all the commotion. Thankfully, he was extremely focused on doing a three-point turn in the middle of this suburban street. I found it odd since he could have just looped around the block. Regardless, he made the turn almost as fast as Austin Powers did in the golf cart scene in *International Man of Mystery*. In the process, he managed to run over an orange cone at the end of the driveway, which made my sister and the kids, who were still watching, laugh pretty hard. I made a mental note about his driving skills.

And we were finally off on the date. He had a perfectly romantic schedule lined up for us. First, we would drive to Alexandria and then hop on a ferry to cross the Potomac to the National Harbor. We would explore the area and grab a bite before heading back. I thought this was wonderful, and was excited for great company on what was sure to be a lovely date. I wondered what my sister would think when she saw my location in her stalker app to be in the middle of the Potomac River! I laughed to myself.

As we were driving to Alexandria, I couldn't help but notice that Doc McPilot was not the smoothest driver. He was doing little herky-jerky things with the wheel, which was fine if it was only once in a while, but he was doing it almost every three seconds. I felt like I was constantly bopping around in the passenger seat from right to left. It didn't get much better when he tried to park his SUV in an incredibly tiny parking garage. I had to get out of the car and observe the production, which took a solid five minutes. I simultaneously thought two things: I hope we don't miss the ferry and I'm glad he's a pilot, not a race car driver.

We made it in time for the ferry. It was a beautiful day, the water was calm, and the sun still shining. We were hitting it off again just like we did on the first date. I asked him if I could guess his birthday and he says yes. I wanted to say February 19 but instead I say February 17. His birthday is February 19. I wondered if perhaps I was psychic or if we had some kind of soulmate connection going on.

Over the next few hours we ate and drank entirely too much, laughing the whole time. I was enjoying his company, yet, for some reason that I can't quite understand, I couldn't help thinking that he wasn't "The One" for me. I found this confusing. I couldn't put my finger on why I thought this since he was obviously a catch, but it seemed that was what my overly indulged gut was telling me.

After dinner, he took me on the Ferris wheel and kissed me at the top. He was an excellent kisser, but we all knew that was going to be the case. As we swayed in the Ferris wheel over two hundred feet in the air, he then told me he had a confession to make.

Oh shit, this sounded ominous. Thank God my sister was stalking me.

He told me that the day before he had matched with a friend of mine as well. I was relieved that was his confession but I was also a bit confused. I didn't even live in DC so how could he know who my friends were around there? It turned out that one of my profile pics was of me and two friends at a Nationals game. My single, local friend put the same pic on her profile as well and the two of them matched.

I gave him a bit of an inquisition. Had they gone out? Did he think she's cute? Why didn't he go out with her instead of me since she actually lived here?

He didn't have any real answers other than that he enjoyed our first date and wanted a second. I felt really guilty. Here I was, playing the field in different states and stealing DC's most eligible bachelor from my dear friend. On top of that, something had told me that he wasn't "The One" but I would selfishly like to continue seeing him. I was torn, however, because I also loved my friend and if I'm being honest, they would probably totally hit it off if they went out. Shoot, what a predicament. What's a girl to do?

I made an earnest attempt to convince him that maybe he should go out with her since I am not moving to DC anytime soon. He and I could just be friends and that I'll give a toast at their wedding, which was bound to happen since they were both clearly wonderful people. Since I was on a roll, I also say that I enjoyed his company but am not sure we were each other's end-all and be-all. He thought I was a bit wackadoo for making that assessment and the suggestion to be friends.

He told me that, while my friend was very cute, he wouldn't go out with her until he saw what would happen with us. <Note to reader: insert heart melting emoji.>

I figured I couldn't argue with that nor did I really want to. So, I let it be and we decided to see each other when I was back in town again.

I came back into town the following month for the Marine Corps

Marathon. A few things happened since our Ferris wheel ferry date. I lined up a new job and quit my old one. And, I found a lump. Yeah, you know what I'm talking about. I found a lump.

First of all, why hadn't any of my dates found this lump? I guess they had been distracted by other things. Whatever. Add that to the list of why dating is so pointless. Thanks for nothing, all you Tinder dates! Well, I found it and by the time I was back in DC, I had already seen my primary care doctor. She said it was probably nothing but that I should get a mammogram and an ultrasound just to be sure. I was mostly put at ease but anxious to get this all wrapped up before I started my new job.

While in DC after the marathon, Doc McPilot and I made plans to grab a bite out so that I could consume all the calories that I had burned that day and then some. We decided to get pizza in Crystal City. Yet again, we had a wonderful time.

I decided to tell Doc McPilot, who I had started to trust as a person and as an almost-doc given how obviously brilliant he is, about my lump. Just like my doc, he told me to get a mammogram and ultrasound, but he also offered to check it out himself with a sly grin on his face. I laughed but didn't say no. I also didn't say yes since, well, we're in a pizza joint.

As we're leaving it starts to rain, and it's getting dark. I decided on the drive back to my sister's house that I actually would like his medical assessment of my lump. *Why not*, I think? It was dark and the people in the cars next to us wouldn't see especially with their windshield wipers going. Doc McPilot eagerly obliged.

Now, let's remember that this was literally the hottest doctor-pilot combo on the planet in front of me, about to perform what could quite possibly be the only medically necessary breast exam in my entire existence that I would actually enjoy. There were no fluorescent lights blinding me as I lay on a paper sheet in a robe that doesn't cover me, while an older woman with cold hands makes the rounds. No, I was in a dark and cozy car with a handsome possible soulmate about to use his manly hands to make a medical assessment that could save my life.

But I couldn't enjoy it. At all.

I couldn't enjoy it because it was dark and raining and Doc McPilot was a horrible driver. I realized that my timing to ask for this exam was awful. We were on a busy road and he was doing his exam while we darted back and forth in the lane. The wipers were going like crazy. There was a red light up ahead but we didn't slow down. I should have had a big smile on my face, but instead I was terrified. I had a death-like, white-knuckle grip on the door handle praying to a God that I didn't believe in that I wouldn't die.

He finished his exam. We survived. And then he said exactly what my doc had. It was probably a fibroadenoma or a cyst, which would be nothing to worry about, but it was best to get a mammogram and ultrasound to be sure. For whatever reason, I trusted him and I promised to keep him posted.

Two weeks later I was diagnosed with breast cancer. Sorry, this isn't a funny paragraph. But I will say that one of the first people I reached out to was Doc McPilot. He took time out of his busy day to talk to me about it and showed me that he clearly cared. I can now see that our meeting was for a reason.

Over the next two months of my treatment journey and ultimate surgery, Doc McPilot and I stayed in contact even though I didn't have time to make it back to DC. He was there for me as a friend and I was incredibly grateful. I'd like to think that I was there for him as a friend too as he figured out the next phase of his life. It turned out that we had a lot in common and both found comfort in picking up the phone and calling the other when we needed a dose of reality.

After my surgery, I asked Doc McPilot if he could give his medical assessment of "the girls," or "the upgrade," as I call them. Thank goodness for the digital era. Doc McPilot was able to do a telehealth appointment with me and give his official medical opinion and it was all good. He said it was better than all good, in fact, and I felt emotionally relieved.

A month or so later, Doc McPilot hopped on a plane to the Middle East where he was leading some super secret squirrel missions for a few months. I hadn't seen him in person since I almost died in his car, but the universe aligned with his layover in Rhode Island. I made my way down to see him from Boston, met his crew, and got to wish him well on his deployment.

Doc McPilot and I kept in touch in between his crazy missions, the time difference, and my new job obligations. We FaceTimed and sent pics. He's such a perfectly wonderful human being and I was so thankful he was in my life. I know that whoever he ends up with will be incredibly lucky.

When he got back to the states, he ended up moving to another state for his residency. The universe aligned again a few months later and we were able to meet up during one of my business trips in his new city. We picked up right where we left off.

At the time of this writing, Doc McPilot and I haven't spoken in about six months, but I know one of these days one of us will reach out to the other. I'll send him this story and make sure he knows that he came into my life for a reason during a scary time for me, and for that I'm so thankful. I will also remind him to ensure autopilot is always on, just in case.

# F*** THE DATING APPS

## GIVE ME YOUR BEST PICKUP LINE.

n the summer of 2019, I got sick and tired of the apps. I was done. Like really done. I had been on most of the big ones and paid their subscription for premium access, which I believed would be the best use of my time and money. I still had nothing to show for it other than a lot of content for some dating bedtime stories that I'm writing here. *Where the heck was my Prince Charming,* I kept wondering? Because he sure as hell wasn't showing up in my match queue.

Like the old saying goes: The definition of insanity is doing the same thing over and over again and expecting a different result. I was shifting from one app to another and darting from one corner of the metro area to the other just to meet new guy after new guy.

It was a significant investment of my precious time, effort, and money. All the apps turned out to be like a Venn diagram; the same people floating from one app into the next. The result was always the same—me coming up empty-handed.

So, to solve this life problem, I decided to dig deep into my creative mind and come up with a creative solution. The opposite of insanity! I first needed to understand the end result I wanted to achieve which, simply put, was to meet someone special.

In order to get there, I had to go on what felt like a million dates. The guys usually looked nothing like their pics or I otherwise felt no connection. I tend to know immediately if I like someone or not. I was wasting a great deal of time going about it the new "traditional" way of dating. Therefore, the real problem was that I was wasting my time on dead-end dates. What I needed was a magical connection to just appear while I was living my life and doing nondating things.

Once I identified the root of the problem, I quickly thought of a solution. I needed the opposite of a wedding ring! I needed a dating flare, quite literally, that made it apparent to random people passing by that I was single and ready to mingle. Just as a wedding band is meant to deter an impromptu, flirtatious interaction, my flare would encourage it.

Perhaps I would wear this flare by the mangoes in the grocery store's produce section, or out for a drink with a friend, or even just sitting on a park bench watching the sunset. In my mind, I imagined that Prince Charming would walk past me and be instantly attracted to me (now, in my mind, I also had perfectly coiffed hair, long eye lashes, and a meticulously put together outfit).

Then Prince Charming would wish he could hit on me, but because that's not normal to do anymore in the world of dating apps, his heart would sink with regret. But then he notices my flare and thinks to himself, *"Wow! This bold and unapologetic beauty is in fact single and there is no way I can give up an opportunity to speak to her. I feel so lucky in this moment!"*

After he finally catches his breath from how stunning I am in the glistening glow of the sunset, he continues to say in his head, *"Thank God. I am so tired of the dead-ends in the dating apps. I just want to find a secure woman who doesn't play games. And here she is, right in front of me. I'm going to hit on her! Here we go . . . "*

And just like that, Prince Charming and I meet in an actual human to human interaction reminiscent of 1999.

Of course, the major risk with this approach is that I would get hit on by people that I'm not at all interested in. But how was that any different than what I had been already doing? The difference was that I would not be wasting my time! Short of collecting all of my app queue members and telling them to show up at a gymnasium on Tuesday at 6:00 p.m. with a name tag so I can rotate through a two minute speed dating session, I needed to severely reduce the time I spent figuring out if I was going to have a connection with someone.

After much discussion with some friends, I decided my flare of choice would be a homemade shirt. A nicely fitting T-shirt that could be dressed up or down. And maybe I would also make a cute tank top version of it to wear at the gym . . . you know, because guys check out girls there anyway.

I found a T-shirt-making website and quickly slapped something together that reads in a large font over the chest area, "F*** THE DATING APPS." In a smaller font below, it said, "Give me your best pickup line." On the back, in a small and tasteful font, was "I'm single and I mingle."

I designed and bought one T-shirt and one tank top for entirely too much money. A couple weeks later, my shirts arrived, and I tried them on. Hmm, the T-shirt was a bit too tight . . . but then again that could work in my favor. The tank top fit fine.

I now ran into a new problem. I had been talking some big game with all my friends about my new idea. I was thinking I could start a business that could really take off! All the single people who complain about dating apps, which is literally all of them, would now have a solution that costs less than what one month of a premium app subscription would! It was genius!

But my problem was that I was too chicken shit to actually wear the thing in public. Did I really want someone to hit on me while in line at the post office? Did I want people staring at my chest in order to read the purposefully placed bold text?

Fortunately, I had a girl's weekend quickly approaching, which would be a safe environment for me to test out the goods.

One long weekend in Savannah, twelve of my loveliest lady friends graced me with their presence. I organized this trip because I wanted to celebrate the wonderful relationships I had in my life, and I was beyond humbled by the number of ladies who wanted to join the festivities.

One of the events I planned for that weekend was to rent out a party bike for a pedal pub tour of Savannah. I decided my F*** the Dating Apps T-shirt was a no brainer for this event! Pedaling through all Savannah and drinking in every pub would maximize my exposure to subjects of interest. I would get a good feel if this would work or not.

We put on our cutest outfits and headed out for a pregame drink before the official imbibing and pedaling began. We all joked about my T-shirt and wondered what pickup lines I would get.

When we arrived at the pedal pub staging area, we greeted our tour guide, Jim, who was already waiting for us in the giant bike. He helped us get settled into our seats and then instructed us on how the whole night was going to go down. We were the engine behind this contraption, so we had to pedal and brake when necessary.

We would be pedaling to each pub on the hit list and stay for as long as we liked. There were more pubs than we could visit in one night but he recommended the sequence of stops and at which one we should end the night. One of my friends hooked up her phone to play some obnoxiously loud 1990s hip-hop and we were off to embarrass ourselves on the streets of Savannah!

Perhaps you're wondering about this Jim guy. Let me describe him for you. He seemed to be pretty tall, although I couldn't really tell because he was sitting down. He had dark hair that was tucked under a beanie and had an attractive face. He was also pretty funny and easygoing. He was one part hipster and one part Rico Suave. He joked with us and we joked back. Even the married ladies in the group were a bit flirty with him, but it was all for fun.

As the organizer of this event, Jim gave me special attention. I assumed this was what he did as a pedal pub tour guide—bachelor-ette parties and the like were probably his biggest hunting ground. Mind you, I was sure to flirt with him and show him my specially designed T-shirt. He laughed at it but didn't use a pickup line on me, surprisingly. I wasn't worried. It didn't keep me from flaunting my chest all over the place especially as the drinks flowed.

After pub #5, I was pretty tipsy and one of the first to saunter back to the pedal bike. Jim, who had been sitting in the bike waiting for us to return, said to me, "It seems I lost my phone number. Can I have yours?"

I was totally confused. "What are you talking about? That makes no sense. You mean you lost your phone?" He started to laugh. I'm even more confused. Why is he laughing if he lost his phone? That shit be expensive. So I asked, "Do you want to use my phone? Hold on, let me find it."

I started to rummage through my fanny pack to find my phone. Yes, I was proudly wearing a fanny pack! Functional and fashionable!

Damn it! I couldn't find my phone. I checked my pockets. Nothing. Where the hell was my phone?

My sister came out of the pub then and said, "Hey, drunk lady! You left your phone on the table inside the bar," as she handed me my phone, thank goodness.

I turned back to Jim. "So do you need my phone?"

Poor Jim was still laughing at me (not with me, mind you). He pointed at my chest and said, "I was doing as your shirt instructed. That was quite obviously a pickup line."

Oh, silly me! It seemed my shirt actually did work as intended and I was too oblivious to even make good use of it! Lesson learned.

I can't remember how I attempted to salvage the rest of that conversation, but eventually he said to me, "No, really, I would like your phone number." So, between pub #5 and #6, Jim got my phone number.

After pub #7, the tour finally came to an end, but the party wasn't. Jim said that he would love to continue to show us the hot spots and we all gladly took him up on his offer. And that's when Jim stepped off the pedal bike.

OMG, he was like 6'5" at least! That was more than a foot taller than me! How the hell did such a tall dude fit in such a small bike seat for four hours? It didn't seem physically possible. Perhaps I was more drunk than I realized because I couldn't seem to make sense of it.

The evening progressed and was a ton of fun. Probably one of the most fun evenings I had in my adult life. We, including Jim, went to a nightclub in a tree house, then did karaoke, which was followed by more drinking and dancing our little hearts out.

Of course, Jim and I were hitting it off. He was a great dancer! We danced well together, despite the height difference.

During the course of the night, my friends were sure to tell every guy they saw to read my T-shirt. That night a lot of guys used pickup lines on me. Some were really good, others absolutely horrific. I realized that my dating flare served a secondary purpose. It could screen the intellect and humor of a guy based on their pickup line. Did they toe the line of impropriety, and did I like it? Did they like a good pun? Or were they stumbling, bumbling idiots when it came to hitting on a girl the old school way? A pickup line says a lot, and, damn it, there's nothing wrong with an unexpected cheesy line that can make you laugh.

Sometime later in the night, Jim took off his beanie and down fell long, gorgeous locks. Yes, you read that correctly. Jim's hair was longer than mine! He wore it well, but I realized that it was probably not going to end well for the two of us because of it. We flirted, made out a little on the dance floor, and had a general great time. Jim even got a bit jealous when guys fed me their pickup lines. Who knew this would be so much fun?

When the night ended around 2:30 a.m., Jim was an absolute gentleman with me and my friends. He ensured we all got home safely, and of course, invited me over but I politely declined. I just couldn't get past all that hair. I know, superficial as it may seem, but it's just not my thing. Poor Jim. I think he had fun even if his pickup line didn't turn into a happy ending.

The next day, those of us who stuck around for another afternoon decided to take a self-guided tour of Savannah and see the sites that we hadn't had a chance to check out yet. We were wandering around a random part of town when all of a sudden we spot Jim! What on earth are the chances?

Jim, the ultimate gentleman, came over and made easy conversation with us. It seemed he was leaving the gym and happened to be heading in the same direction as us. He offered to give us a mini walking tour of that part of town, and we accepted.

Now, you can't make this shit up. It was like we were in some goddamn rom-com. At the corner of Jones Street, from the phrase "Keeping up with the Joneses," we saw an old lady walking a pug. We all started oohing and aahing over this little guy. But the pug got off his leash somehow and started running directly into the street! We all started to scream in fear!

Jim took off after him! Our hero, Jim, with those long legs of his, was able to easily catch up with the pug. He scooped up the pug in one smooth movement and walked back to us while cradling the pug in his arms like a small baby. Literally, the entire gaggle of girls started oohing and aahing over Jim. It happened so fast that we didn't get a picture or video, but I assure you that this moment is forever ingrained in all our minds.

We eventually made it to a beautiful fountain and took a group pic with Jim. He told us that we were in the top three of the best groups he had given a tour to. We felt honored, yet slighted that we weren't the top group. He said we were beat out by a bachelor party that didn't stop going until dawn. We can admit defeat to that.

It was time for Jim to head back on his merry way. None of us wanted him to leave, because how would the rest of the story go without our male protagonist? He started to walk off when my cousin yells after him, "Don't look back! Just go! Please don't look back, we can't take it!"

But Jim did look back at us, as if he too felt the strong cords that connected us from this fabulous weekend. We laughed and cried simultaneously in this moment.

The world is a small place. Months later, one of the girls who was on this trip was at work in Chicago talking with a colleague when Savannah came up in discussion. My friend mentioned our girl's trip and of course the pedal tour. Then she mentioned Jim. It turns out this other person also met him! They were able to describe Jim accurately: tall as can be, with long, luscious hair, and a great personality. If you're ever in Savannah, keep an eye out for Jim saving small puppies at busy intersections and ask him if he remembers our crazy group of girls. And then please buy him a drink for us.

# THE FIRST KISS

## IT'S BETTER TO KNOW SOONER RATHER THAN LATER WHETHER HE'S GOING TO BE A PRINCE OR REMAIN A FROG.

When I told my sister I was writing this book, she made me promise that I wouldn't include any of the guys that I was actively dating. I am a woman of my word, so this chapter is included to ensure that I never go out with this guy again.

I went on several dates with a former marine who happened to live about two miles from me. We matched on one of the apps more than once. I remember matching with him at least two times previously. He was handsome, and based on his ex-military status, I also assumed he would be the type of alpha male I find attractive. For whatever reason, our previous communications never went anywhere but into the black hole of dating apps only to then resurface on a new app a few months later. Such is life.

Well, on this particular occasion, we lined up an actual date. We agreed to meet halfway at a cool Asian fusion eatery that had great reviews and interesting cocktails. Perfect.

Our first date went fine. And I mean "fine" like any woman says "fine" but doesn't really mean it. There was nothing super remarkable about it, but also nothing awful. I found him to be fairly attractive and super fit, which helped. We had a good amount in common, other than his choice of military branch to serve. He was an easy conversationalist and I enjoyed myself enough to not have to end the date early. Yes, my standards are very high. I decided during the date that I would go out with him again because, honestly, I had nothing else promising in the queue. I decided to call him Mister Marine.

As we closed out the tab, Mister Marine asked if I would like to go out again. I said yes and we talked about meeting up the next weekend perhaps. Great, this was moving along!

We left the restaurant to go our separate ways and head home. Now, this is usually where a date gets awkward. We had already gotten the next date logistics out of the way, however, it was time to see if he would go in for a kiss or just a hug.

You can tell a lot about a man by the way he says goodbye. On a busy sidewalk, I once had a guy pull me in for a hot kiss tangling my hair in his hands in the process. As he slowly pulled his hands out of my hair, he made intense eye contact with me. Let's just say that guy got a second date for sure and he wasn't even a marine. Needless to say, I had high expectations standing on this curb with Mister Marine, waiting to see if he would lay one on me like he meant it. I thought that that would be the only way this date goes from unremarkable to truly worthy of a second one.

Here it comes. He leans in . . . and gives me a gentle hug.

I think, *What? Really? Okay. Maybe I should cut him a break and assume he's just being a gentleman. I'm sure he'll go in for the real thing on date number two, which is around the corner anyway. No biggie.*

The week goes by, and we exchanged a few texts. The usual, "How was your day" conversations that put me to sleep. The more days that pass, it seemed the less interested I became in this guy. Where was the alpha male? Why didn't we have firm plans for the weekend?

That Saturday afternoon, I returned home from a second date with another guy. I was putting my feet up on the couch, reclining into what would be a perfect evening with my cat, and getting ready to dig into a pint of homemade vegan ice cream, when I get a ding on my phone, and see Mister Marine has left a message. It seems he wants to know what I was up to that night.

Now, I am all about being spontaneous and fun, but I also want to feel that a guy is excited about me and can't wait to line up the next date. We had gone a whole week with meaningless texts only for Mister Marine to try to line something up last minute. As if he thinks I am at home with my cat on a Saturday night. That may be true, but it's rude nonetheless!

I punted the date to Sunday afternoon. We'd go for a long walk around the Seaport District and stop for a drink and apps some-where. Great, that was taken care of. I could now get back to couch potato status.

I assumed my usual position on the couch, which involved fully stretching out with my electronic devices, TV remote, and needless calories all within easy reach. Then my sweet little cat made her way onto the couch to assume her usual position on my chest, her furry face inches from mine.

On this Saturday evening, we both got very comfy. She sat as if she was laying an egg on my chest and put her little nose up to my nose. I cupped her little head in my hands and closed the distance, making our noses touch. Then, since my head is larger than her head, my lips were able to kiss her little chinny chin chin. And I proceeded to give her no less than one hundred very soft and loving kisses on her little chinny chin chin, maybe the occasional cheek, while I whispered how much I loved her into her little ears. It was beautiful, really.

Yes, I'm a crazy cat lady who made out with her cat. I'm not at all ashamed about it.

All right, back to my story about Mister Marine.

He and I met up the next day. He made fine conversation. After a few miles, I start to get really hungry so we decide to stop at Hopsters in the Seaport District. Pumpkin spice cider was on the menu and, given the chilly fall weather, I think it's a perfect choice. Mister Marine orders it too.

If you winced when reading he ordered the same drink as me, don't worry, I did too. At this point, I had no doubt about the fact that Mister Marine was not an alpha. Yet, I found myself hoping that after a couple of ciders, he would find his manly ways and lay one on me. Really, that was the only reason I was hanging in there.

After a few drinks and some appetizers, we wrapped things up and headed back outside. I checked the time and realized it was only seven o'clock. My bedtime wasn't for another hour, which left plenty of time to make out like high schoolers. Let's see how this played out, shall we?

Mister Marine offered to walk me most of the way to my place, which was very gentlemanly of him. He announced that he was going to turn left at the upcoming intersection.

*FINALLY*, I think. He's going to kiss me, and I can determine whether there will be a third date.

When we got to the intersection, things suddenly got super awkward. He just looked at me. I was probably not helping matters because I noticed we were standing under a very bright streetlight with four cars stopped at the traffic light right next to us. This was not a very private place to give a goodnight kiss. Mind you, I didn't necessarily need privacy. I just needed to know if there was going to be a third date or not.

He leaned in . . . and gave me a hug.

WTF.

I said, "Okay, well I had a nice time. Enjoy your evening," and walked off.

He replied while chasing after me, "You know what? I will walk you two more blocks."

*OMG,* I thought. *We were going to have to do the awkward goodbye AGAIN?!* Deep breath. Maybe, just maybe, he realized he missed his chance, and he would kiss me, finally.

We walked two blocks down to an even busier intersection where the streetlight was twice as bright, and there was even less privacy for a romantic goodnight kiss. But, whatever, I no longer cared. I just wanted the goddamn kiss, please.

He leaned in, with an awkward look on his face again, and . . . gave me another hug.

*I can't. I just can't,* I think. I said goodbye, while smirking uncontrollably, and headed toward home. I talked to myself all the way home about what a colossal waste of time dating this guy was, which was very rude, I know, blaming it on the pumpkin spice ciders.

On the positive side, I salvaged the rest of my evening and was able to get in bed with my cat before nine o'clock.

The next week, Mister Marine engaged me in more of the same meaningless text conversations. I found myself having trouble remembering his actual name. That's how little I cared. The weekend arrived and I chose Saturday evening to stuff my face with home-made pizza while watching a rom-com.

Mister Marine texted me while I was eating and asked if I watched UFC. What? I get that I'm ex-military, but what about me could possibly make someone think that men fighting in a cage is my television pastime of choice? I politely told him that I never go out of my way to watch UFC. Then he asked me what I was up to.

Déjà vu. I let the text sit there for fifteen minutes because I was annoyed. I finally responded and said that I was eating dinner and watching a movie. I was even so bold as to say that if he was planning on inviting me that evening to watch a UFC fight with him, I was not planning on leaving my apartment.

He responded that he wasn't going to watch the UFC fight. Then why the hell did he ask me about it? I didn't know what was going on. However, in the back of my head, I was thinking that I still wanted to know if this guy was a good kisser. He was one of the more fit dudes I'd been out with recently and I fully recognized that I had already invested enough time in him that I might as well go on one more date. Sunk cost fallacy for sure.

I suggested that we hang out the next afternoon, perhaps watch the Patriots game. He agreed.

The next day, we were watching the game at his place, which was incredibly nice. I was legitimately impressed. He mentioned that he bought some drinks for me and offers me a White Claw. <insert eye roll> I prefer the unexpected, like a High Noon or something less millennial! Regardless, I had a couple of them.

In person, his conversation was fine, again, but I was fully expecting him to just lean over and kiss me. Halftime came and went. The second half of the game came and went. Seven o'clock rolled around and the much anticipated political interview that I had actual interest in watching was coming on. I just would have preferred to do it on my couch with my cat since clearly this dude wasn't going to kiss me. I was officially over the date and wanted to scurry out of there so I could make it home in time to catch the interview.

I stood up and, with my left hand, picked up my remaining White Claw, a napkin, and my phone. I said, "Thank you for having me over," and I announced that I was leaving.

Mister Marine popped up with a sudden burst of energy and quickly walked over to me. It seemed he would be finally kissing me! Thank God! Yet there I was, standing with my trash and phone in hand! Not really the best timing. Whatever, let's just do this!

He leaned in slowly, very slowly. He pursed his lips and kissed my lips. I barely felt it.

I think, *What's going on here? Is he kissing me? Or is there a strong breeze going through his condo that I just happen to feel only on my lips?*

I opened my eyes to get a peek. Oh, no, he was definitely up in my grill and doing what is his best impression of kissing.

He did it again. This incredibly soft and gentle kiss. And again. And again.

Meanwhile, I was still holding my trash in my left hand. The interview I desperately wanted to watch was now playing on the TV. I wondered if he was just warming up like a Ferrari needing to get its engine going.

It seems he wanted to continue doing whatever it was he was doing. I opened my eyes again to make sure there was still a human in front of my face. I was slightly disappointed when I realized that he was still there. I found myself wishing that it was just a figment of my imagination.

I decided I needed to not focus on what was happening as he "warmed up." Using my right hand, which was otherwise awkwardly hanging there, I decided to explore. The guy was fairly fit so maybe I could see what else he had going on to assess whether this encounter would continue around more bases. I explored for a minute. Yes, he was fit. It was a shame he kissed like a wimp.

We were at least three minutes into these butterfly kisses when my left arm got tired of holding my trash up in the air. I was done exploring so I started to watch the interview on TV with my open left eye.

Then it hit me.

OMG, he was kissing me like I kiss my cat! Is this what my cat feels when I smother her with butterfly kisses?

I started to laugh. I, honest to God, started to laugh. I don't know what was going on and who taught this guy to make out with a woman, but this sure as hell wasn't doing anything for me. In fact, it was actually making me wish I was home with my cat. At least she purrs when I kiss her. This guy wasn't making a peep, which, on second thought, I don't mind since it allowed me to hear the interview better.

You know what? I can't fucking do this anymore.

I broke away and put down the trash. I decided I needed to teach this almost-forty-year-old man how to kiss a woman. And that's exactly what I did.

I believe I managed to salvage the remainder of the evening while still catching most of the interview. However, I was scarred from the butterfly kisses and couldn't do it again. Part of me felt bad since there was really nothing wrong with him other than he was a poor kisser.

I also realized that there was no point in seeing him again. I could make out with my cat any night of the week and twice on Sunday. I may be a crazy cat lady but that doesn't mean I have to kiss my date like one.

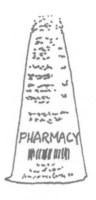

# MY ONE, ONE NIGHT STAND

## HOW I RANG IN THE NEW YEAR WITH A BANG.

"How Christie Got Her Groove Back" might as well be the story line to my weeklong vacation in Puerto Rico. It was fall 2019 and my one-year anniversary of being cancer-free was approaching. To celebrate life, I decided to plan a holiday somewhere I had never been and spend my anniversary day, December 26, on a beach showing off the new girls.

Mind you, I had just come off a tremendous girl's weekend with twelve other fabulous ladies. I had never been on a nonwork trip completely solo. The only thing that had come close was a trip to the Grand Caymans I won through work that my idiot ex declined to join me on, a decision that proved to be the final straw in a crumbling relationship.

recap that trip to the Grand Caymans since it was
 in my spinster journey.

inning an incredible work award, I arrived at the
lton in 2017 at the expense of my employer. I was
excited ous to be there. How would I survive one week
surrounded by 150 other winners and work colleagues, all of whom
had a guest with them? I was the only one who was pathetic enough
to travel alone.

I vividly remember checking in to the hotel and entering my room.
It was beautiful and luxurious. Literally everything you could imagine
for a beachfront 5-star hotel in an exotic location.

But I was alone and felt it. I walked into that gorgeous room,
dropped my suitcase by the door, and collapsed, face down, into
the Egyptian cotton duvet on the oversized king bed.

Then, I just cried. I cried about how lonely I felt. I cried about
how embarrassed I was to have a successful professional life but
a bad romantic one. I cried at the anxiety of having to explain to
everyone I was going to see from work that I couldn't find a single
person to go on this trip with me. I cried because I felt lost. I cried,
and I cried, and I cried.

Eventually, I ran out of things to cry about. The emotions felt so
real, but soon I just laid there in silence. Still face down, mind you.
Perhaps I was hoping to asphyxiate in the 700-thread count sheets,
I don't know.

I also don't know how long I laid there, face down, in the bed. It
was enough to make a small puddle of tears, but not long enough
that anyone sent out a search party for me.

Eventually, I pulled myself off the bed and unpacked my clothes,
consciously telling myself through deep breaths that I was lucky
to be there. That I deserved to be there. And that if the asshole I
dated for a decade couldn't see how great I was, then that was his

problem not mine. He was back in Boston packing up his shit and I was in paradise on the company's dollar. Who got the long end of this stick? Me, motherfucker.

Feeling empowered, I put on my bathing suit and chic cover up, grabbed sunglasses to hide my bloodshot eyes, and walked right out of my hotel room.

I am so proud of myself for what came next. Despite the feelings of loneliness and emptiness that were hiding in the shadows, I walked proudly straight out to the beach. I sat down on a beach chair and gave myself a figurative hug. Then I looked around. This place was absolutely stunning. Wow.

*I am proud to be here*, I told myself. *I am okay. I am better than okay, in fact. And I'm going to enjoy the hell out of this free vacation if it's the last goddamn thing I ever do.*

When a server came by, I ordered a ginormous hummus and veggie platter and balanced it out with a sugar-rich piña colada.

I kept my promise to myself and didn't cry again while there. In fact, I ended up having the time of my life, becoming close friends with a colleague and her sister. I recognized that no one cared if I was alone or not. They didn't see me as a failure like I saw myself. No, they saw me as a winner. Because this was a winner's trip!

Fast forward to 2019 when I decided to spend my one-year cancer free anniversary in Puerto Rico showing off my upgraded girls. While in theory I figured I could enjoy the trip alone, I also felt it might be fun to invite a companion to join me.

I had invited a few of the guys I had been dating in the months leading up to the trip, but had no takers.

I had invited all the ladies who went to Savannah with me, but had no takers.

I started to wonder if no one wanted to go with me because there was something wrong with going to Puerto Rico? Did I book the wrong paradise vacation spot?

Then I legit started to get nervous. Clearly, there was something wrong. Why couldn't I find a travel buddy in six months? With desperation and anxiety brewing at almost full strength, I sent out an open invitation to pretty much everyone I knew, who also wouldn't annoy the hell out of me should we spend a week together, for this trip.

Still, I had no takers.

Oh God, how pathetic.

Well then, the universe must not have wanted anyone to go on this trip with me. Maybe, with this new sense of spirituality I had started to develop over the past two years, I should have just practiced what I supposedly believed. It was time to stop trying to control an outcome and just trust in the universe.

With the help of my trusted therapist, I devised a plan so I could truly enjoy this paradise vacation. Since I respond well to goals, especially in difficult times, I developed three objectives to strive to accomplish each day of my Puerto Rican solo trip.

The first goal was to do something nice for myself every day, like taking a bubble bath, getting a massage, or treating myself to a huge piece of chocolate cake for dessert. It wouldn't matter what, it just needed to be for and about me.

The second was to work out and mediate every day; to exercise the body and calm the mind so I could feel grounded and healthy inside and out.

The final goal was terrifying. I promised myself that I was going to truly come out of my shell and become comfortable in the uncomfortable. I would not only talk to friendly strangers, but I would like it. I hoped.

I most definitely had an anxiety attack as I packed for Puerto Rico. This was going to be uncharted territory for me. I had traveled so much for work, often solo even when going overseas, but there were always people I knew for at least part of the trip. Never had I ever been alone in my own head for an entire week. What if I get to my room and just lie on the bed and cry like I did in the Grand Caymans?

I arrived at my beautiful beachfront hotel in San Juan and noticed that my anxiety had long since dissipated. Although the moment of truth would be when I eventually step into my hotel room. Would I face-plant into the bed and throw a pity party?

Uh oh. Rachelle at the front desk tells me that my room wasn't ready yet.

I think to myself, *Wait a second. Oh my God, this is amazing. I can't face-plant into my bed because I can't get to my bed! Rachelle thinks I'm a crazy person because I'm smiling ear to ear.*

I decided to get directions to the bathroom so I could change into my bikini and find the pool bar.

*Here we go,* I think.

The grounds were beautiful and the picturesque pool bar was the perfect place to test out my trip goals. I chose to sit at the corner seat and order a spicy margarita.

Well, this was awkward. What was I supposed to look at? I wondered if I should stare at the football game I don't care about on the TV just to avoid awkward eye contact? How should I make conversation with perfect strangers without being a creep? How could I try not to look pathetic with my giant and uncertain eyes darting all over the place?

I don't think I ever found the answer to these questions, but it really doesn't matter. While I was sitting there, I just started to smile. There I was, in paradise. I was doing it! I was doing it solo and I was okay with it.

I took a selfie and sent it to some family and friends back home. I felt connected to them but I didn't feel that I needed them. I found myself beginning to feel strangely confident in the unknown of the week.

A woman who looked to be about my age sat down next to me. She was alone as well. At one point, our eyes met, and I decided to just go for it. I asked how she was enjoying her stay at the hotel so far.

And just like that, a conversation started. I learned that she was from Dominica, a country I had never heard of before, and that she was on her way to California to visit a friend for a few weeks. I found her confidence in solo travel both intriguing and contagious.

She asked me what I had planned for the week and I told her that I hadn't scheduled any excursions or activities yet. I didn't tell her that my anxiety leading up to the trip had left me functionally paralyzed in this department. However, I did ask her if she had any recommendations on what I should do while there.

During that conversation with a perfect stranger whose name I never learned, she told me about an app that allows you to schedule paid professional experiences with locals. I had to get on there and check out all the cool things to do at the drop of a hat.

I took her advice and logged in. Within thirty minutes, I booked a trip into the rainforest as well as surfing lessons. I saw several other activities that I couldn't wait to read more about. Wow, my week had just gotten a whole lot more exciting!

Maybe I would have figured out on my own how to book activities, or with the help of the hotel concierge, separate websites, or perhaps I would have stumbled upon the app myself, but I thanked my new fast friend for her advice and told her that I think she changed the trajectory of my trip.

No, it was larger than that. I learned a lot about myself in that first hour of my trip. I learned that the world is not as scary as I had made it out to be. That people are friendly more often than they are not. That, when you are open to it, the universe gives you exactly what you need. You just have to open your ears and eyes.

My week was nothing short of incredible. I enjoyed my surfing lesson so much that I took another later in the week. I was even able to stand up on the board, holding my own on these baby waves.

While returning from lessons I came across a giant iguana. I asked a stranger to take a picture of me and my little, but big friend.

If I hadn't ventured out to try something different that morning, what would I have experienced in my comfort zone? Maybe nothing, I don't know. I was thankful for the universe in continuing to bring me new experiences.

I ventured on my own to the town of Old San Juan, perusing random stores along cobblestone streets before I happened upon the place where the piña colada was invented. I sat at the bar by myself, with the newfound confidence I learned from my beautiful Dominican friend.

While drinking that piña colada, I chatted up a large group of Americans who were sitting next to me. They were celebrating a fiftieth birthday. At times, I sat in my seat perfectly content in my own silence. While at other times, I spoke with someone in their group, or they started talking to me. It wasn't weird or awkward. It was lovely.

On a whim, I decided to experience something new—a burlesque performance in the hotel I was staying at. I didn't know what to expect at all. Preshow, I was sitting by myself in this strange and small theater and felt a twinge of awkwardness sitting there quietly while everyone around me otherwise engaged in conversation. Two seats were open next to me and a gorgeous blonde woman and her man approached and asked me if they could take those seats. Of course I welcomed them.

A moment later, the woman started to talk to me. And just like that, I made yet another friend. I learned that she and her boyfriend were from DC on a mini vacation and that her two daughters would be arriving the next day to join them. The three of us talked so much

I barely noticed that the lights had dimmed and the show was about to begin. And what a show it was.

The next night, I booked group salsa lessons. It didn't matter that I was alone, there was sure to be another single person to be my dance partner.

Before heading to the salsa lessons, I decided to grab a drink at the hotel lobby bar, which was under an absolutely magnificent chandelier. There were only a few empty seats open, so I sat down next to a couple.

What do you know, they started talking to me! It doesn't matter, however, because I've long since stopped thinking about if, when, or how to talk to strangers. You just do it.

I learned that this lovely couple lived in DC, just like the couple from the night before, and that this hotel was their favorite vacation spot. The chandelier above us was the third largest chandelier in the world! We stared up at it in awe. How would I have ever known that if I hadn't talked to this couple?

I told them that I was about to head off to get some salsa lessons. They were impressed that I was traveling on my own and eager to experience all my vacation had to offer. I was proud of myself in this moment.

I wished them a lovely rest of their vacation and headed off to my salsa lessons.

My dance partner sweated profusely, but he was pretty good company otherwise. I was able to take away a few basic pointers after an hour of instruction. Then, the whole group hit the town! We were off to practice our new moves with the locals.

There wasn't a single song at the local bar that I sat out. A stranger wanted to take me for a spin across the dance floor every chance there was and I welcomed it.

Eventually, I realized that I had had my fill for one night. I thanked the instructor and my lovely classmates for a great evening before I called a ride back to the hotel.

By day four of my vacation, I was in a groove. Eduardo, who managed the beach chairs for the hotel, and I were on a first name basis. He started reserving some prime front-row seats for me every morning. While lounging under my umbrella in the first row, a couple with a young daughter made their way to the edge of the water. The father, presumably, took a few pictures of the wife and their daughter.

I thought to myself what a shame it is that the father can't be in their family photo. I had asked strangers throughout my week to snap a quick picture of me, which I should mention is driven more by how bad I look in selfies than my newfound comfort in stranger talk.

So, I walked over to the man and asked him if I he would like to be in the picture as well. He was surprised but happy I made the offer. He told me that he hadn't been in many pictures all week. I told him that I was traveling alone and become a pro at asking random people to take a picture of me. The least I could do is return the favor.

Perhaps my favorite activity on this trip was when I joined a group of ten random people for an all-day rainforest hike. The tour guides did an incredible job of hosting us in the wilderness. We saw some remarkable rainforest nooks and crannies that included several waterfalls.

I genuinely enjoyed the company of the entire group. One young woman was also doing a solo trip to celebrate her twenty-fourth birthday. *Holy cow*, I thought. *She is twenty-four and doing what I have just learned to do at thirty-seven.* But you know what, at least I was doing it.

When it came time to swing on a rope or jump off a thirty-five-foot cliff into a mysterious body of water, I was the first one to do it. Our guide told me exactly where to stand and jump. I about peed my pants, but I did it and my new friends screamed with excitement as I flung myself off the rocks and into the abyss.

The day was nothing short of magical. It was so good, in fact, that most of the group wanted to link back up for drinks at a local dive place. I declined. I was ready to spend some time by myself.

How could it be that I no longer dreaded being by myself, but <GASP> I actually welcomed it? How far I had truly come.

That evening while in my hotel room meditating, I felt the room shake for about ten seconds. I assumed, in the moment, that it was vibrations from the music playing in the club off the lobby and reverberating up several floors. The next day, however, I found out that it had been an earthquake. It was the first earthquake of any recognizable magnitude that I had ever experienced. Had I not been still in my room at that time, would I have felt it?

It was my last day in paradise and also New Year's Eve. I had never felt so calm and appreciative of anything in my life than I did in that very moment. How lucky was I to be there? I couldn't wait to experience what the universe had in store for me on this final day.

Eduardo had hooked me up with the best beach chair in the house. I tipped him well and assumed my position for a day filled with nothing but relaxation.

I knew that for New Year's, the hotel was having the biggest party in all of San Juan. Hotel guests could attend for free but would be relegated to a place further away from the stage. The hotel had two big singers hitting the stage: one a Latin Grammy winner and the other a Latin Grammy nominee. The party would be off the charts according to the hotel.

While the party sounded awesome, I hadn't decided what I wanted to do just yet. I'd been playing the week by ear and that evening was no exception. I was at peace with the thought of being asleep at midnight.

I spent the entire day on the beach and in the water, soaking up the sound of the water and the feel of the sun. The sun was about to set and the time had come to leave the beach once and for all.

I was chilly so I made my way to the pool area to warm up in the massive hot tub. There were several people in the hot tub but I was no longer shy. I got right in.

I heard someone call my name and I looked up. It was the blonde bombshell friend I made from the burlesque show! She was in the hot tub with her two daughters. She introduced me to them and said I was the woman she had told them about. Why would someone mention me to their daughters if we only met for a brief moment in time? I didn't know, but was flattered that I had left an impression.

There were others in the hot tub too. They were intrigued by our conversation and started talking as well. I realized that this absolutely gorgeous family was all around me. Why the hell were there so many good looking people in this hot tub?

They were super friendly. The mom and dad were in their late forties at most. Their three drop-dead gorgeous kids were between the ages of twenty-one and twenty-five or so. The adult kids lived in Boston, like me! What a happy coincidence.

They were also incredibly smart, kind, and funny, as being ridiculously good looking wasn't enough. I couldn't figure out which of the two sons was more handsome. It didn't really matter, twenty-five was too young for this thirty-seven-year-old spinster.

Our conversation was great, finding similarities between us all in the hot tub. The ties were uncanny.

Then, as if on cue, the DC couple from the "chandelier bar" swam up to the hot tub! What the hell was going on here? How come everyone I had met in this hotel is now in the hot tub at the same time? The only person missing was Eduardo.

I mentioned that to everyone, and we all had a good laugh.

It was late, though. Eventually, we all needed to get out of the hot tub before becoming supersaturated, wrinkled versions of ourselves.

Someone asked if anyone was going to the lobby party that evening. All eleven people just looked at each other, taking turns saying we weren't sure. Like a high school girl sleepover pact, we decided in unison to meet for drinks at eight o'clock. With that simple suggestion, we all enthusiastically agreed.

Okay, it was time to get primped for my last night in Puerto Rico.

I wore a strappy, colorful little dress. It was way too short for a thirty-seven year old, but then again, I was on vacation and wanted to show off my legs.

Knowing myself and how I tend to be forgetful when tipsy, I decided to forego a purse. Instead, I packed my hotel key, a twenty dollar bill, a credit card, and lip balm into my strapless bra. I looked good and felt even better.

I made my way to the bar right at eight o'clock, meeting the couple from DC under the same chandelier where we first met. The family with beautiful offspring joined us next. We drank, talked, danced, and laughed. We were having a fantastic time before the headliners even hit the stage.

At one point, my DC friend said that there was a couple they wanted to introduce me to. Up walks the family whose picture I took on the beach just a couple of days before! What were the chances I would see them again?

As nonpaying party guests, we had to enjoy the music from a sunken bar area about thirty feet away from the main staging area. Above us was another level that was flush to the stage. Suckers had paid a hundred dollars for a table and bottle service in a roped off area there. Our area wasn't bad yet we joked about how we would have liked to sneak up to the stage anyway.

The mom of the "prime genetics family" said she needed to use the restroom. We wondered if she would be able to sneak to the stage and wished her good luck.

Five minutes later she returned with an empty bladder but no bragging rights.

I was feeling empowered by the couple cocktails I had downed. I also felt in the moment. I had no concerns or worries. I was just *present*.

I announced to the group that I was going to go use the restroom and that I would wave to them when I got near the stage. They all looked at me laughed. Didn't they know that I was living in the flow of the universe? I had no doubts.

As I made my way to the restroom, hotel employees were managing who goes in and out of the high value area, which was surrounded with velvet ropes. I scoped out the joint like I was going to rob it.

When I exited the restroom a few moments later, I decided my best approach was just to walk up like I belonged there. I thought to myself, *Avoid eye contact and just exude confidence.*

Oh my God, it worked. No one stopped me. One server even moved out of the way for me to get by. How was it so easy?

I was able to make my way to the stage. I found my friends down below and waved. They couldn't believe it! They pointed and waved back! Okay, that challenge was now complete.

With the party in full swing, I found myself four rows away from the Latin Grammy nominee.

He scanned the crowed and pulled a lucky young lady from the front row onto the stage. He danced with her for a few seconds then serenaded her with his sexy Latin vocals before sending her back.

I love a good challenge and clearly planned on being the next person pulled up on stage.

Slowly, I snuck through the crowd, making my way to the front row. I found a good spot and enjoyed the accomplishment for the next five minutes. The music was great. I couldn't understand a word but I was dancing and having the time of my life.

Next thing I know, the singer crossed the stage to where I was standing and put his hand out toward me, inviting me up! Ha! Looking back, I can't say that I didn't believe it, but I did. I literally made it happen.

I was on stage, being serenaded, and putting my new salsa moves to good use for a solid thirty seconds. I played hard to get with my moves too. I may have known who he was, Latin Grammy nominee and all, but did he know who I was? I made him work for my attention, damn it.

Everything about that moment was fun. When I had enough, I shook my little booty back off the stage and joined the commoners in the crowd.

My friends had somehow made it to the stage and were going nuts! The oldest son, who we'll call Scott, told me that I had been awesome up there. He wanted to know how I did it. I said that I had decided to make it happen and therefore it did.

Scott's brother had caught the whole thing on camera. Since I didn't have my phone—not everything fit in my bra—he texted the video to me so I could enjoy it later.

Scott and I began to talk. He was very handsome with his dark glasses and ruffled brown hair. He was just under six feet tall and very athletic, which I had noticed in the hot tub earlier that day. In a way, he resembled a young Clark Kent. I could tell by the way he carried himself that he thought of himself as a nerd rather than an athlete. I figured that he was also completely unaware of his incredible good looks. I found everything about him endearing. This guy was going to be a catch for some lucky lady one day.

As the party progressed into the night we became inseparable. I realized that I was an old lady hanging out with someone twelve years my junior, but I didn't really care. We were all adults.

The countdown to 2020 was called out. I couldn't remember the last time anyone kissed me at midnight on New Year's Eve. For a second, I was sad that I still didn't have that someone special in my life. Rather than a kiss on the lips, however, I exchanged a kiss on the cheek with all my new friends. I couldn't have asked for better countdown companions.

The party was still rocking at one o'clock, and the only remaining members of our group were me, Scott, and his brother. We were having so much fun dancing that we didn't notice that the others had called it a night.

Scott's brother had found a Puerto Rican celebrity to dance with while Scott and I tore it up ourselves. He was an excellent dancer. Was there anything this guy was not good at?

At one point I couldn't help myself but ask Scott how old he thought I was. After taking a moment to think about it, he said that, based on my background and looks, he would guess that I was around thirty-one.

I laughed. How cute. I thanked him and said I was thirty-seven. He was surprised but he didn't seem to care. I was relieved.

As the live music ended and a DJ took over, we continued to dance. As the party was about to end, Scott finally pulled me close and kissed me. I knew he had been thinking about it for a while and the wait was worth it. He was adorably handsome and, not surprisingly, an excellent kisser. Clearly, we both were having a wonderful time.

We danced and kissed until the music stopped at two o'clock.

Scott and I just looked at each other wondering what we were supposed to do next. I'd never had a one night stand before. The new me, of being open to the universe and experiences, was not necessarily about sex. I was looking for what helped me to grow as a person versus getting needs met.

Somehow, this felt like it was part of the plan the universe had in store for me. How could it not have been? Up to this point, this trip had been the most incredible week of my life. This night had been one of the most incredible nights of my life.

I felt free. Alive! Grateful for everything, everyone, and everywhere. Nothing was lacking in my life. I was in love with my life. I had come so far the past year. No, more like two and a half years. I was a new person and I felt it in every fiber of my being.

In that moment, I reflected on my past. The emotional and mental trauma from my time in the army, followed by a ten-year unfulfilling, codependent relationship, then a breast cancer diagnosis, all rocked my world many times over. I went through deep bouts of depression sandwiched between crippling anxiety. And, through all of it, I had somehow found myself in the most beautiful headspace. My life couldn't have been any different for the better, and for all that I was aware and grateful.

I asked Scott if he wanted to keep our party going. He most certainly did, but, as I had assumed, he was staying in the same suite as his family.

I tried hard not to smile. Obviously, I had my own room with no family members close by. There was no question. I wasn't going to dare venture into his wing of the hotel. His family was very welcoming toward me, but not *that* welcoming.

Okay then, it was settled. We would go to my room. Assuming this was going to lead to what we thought it would lead to, I asked him if he had protection.

Oh, handsome Clark Kent Junior didn't. Of course he didn't, he was on vacation with his family. But this was Puerto Rico, and we could just walk two blocks to a twenty-four-hour convenience store and pick some up. Off we went, arm in arm, on a romantic walk to CVS, enjoying our conversation the whole way.

At the CVS we made our way to the condom section. Blankly, we both looked at each other. Damn it, he didn't know what to get?

Okay, I was a puma in this dynamic, since I wasn't old enough to be a cougar. I suppose I should handle the situation.

I picked up a box that looked familiar, not knowing what I was buying honestly, and he agreed with my choice. Since I chose them and was holding the box, I figured I might as well pay for them.

At the checkout I dug down into my bra and pulled out my cash. Scott thought this was hilarious. I thought to myself, *Laugh all you want, young man, but if I didn't do that and had lost my purse, you'd be paying for the condoms!*

The cashier handed me the receipt and change, everything except the coins going back into my bra. I gave Scott the coins because I didn't want clinking noises emanating from my bra all the way back to the hotel.

Scott and I avoided eye contact with the hotel staff as we made our way through the empty lobby and to the eleventh floor to my room we go.

In the privacy of my room, I decided to do a little striptease for this handsome creature in front of me. I took off my little strappy dress and waved it around a little while practicing a version of my solo salsa moves. The dress eventually got tossed in the air dramatically.

Next came my bra. Scott was sitting on the bed absolutely mesmerized by this ridiculous striptease.

Just before taking off my bra, I realized I had all that shit shoved in there. That was not going to make for a sexy striptease, which I was in the middle of. *Screw it*, I thought. *I'm going to just pretend it's part of the act.*

I dug into the left side of the bra and grabbed the cash and my lip balm. I swayed my hips, making what I thought was a sultry look, and threw in a little turn. Then I placed the items on the dresser. Okay, one more dig into the bra and then I could move it along.

I reached back into the bra and grabbed what else was left. Oh, it was the receipt. Scott was still sitting there with a giant grin on his face. Either he thought I was so bad that I was good, or he had never seen someone strip before and therefore couldn't tell that I had no idea what I was doing. It didn't matter because it was still fun.

I swayed my hips, did a little turn, made a little face, and then pulled out the receipt.

Oh my God. The receipt! I thought it was a small receipt, but it literally kept going and going! Like a magician pulling a scarf out of their sleeve. The world's longest CVS receipt kept coming and coming, one coupon at a time, from my bra.

My sexy face turned to one of confusion and shock. I was so distracted by the receipt that I stopped my sensual moves. I used both hands to pull the forty feet of paper out of my cleavage. This was not part of the choreography for the evening. I looked at Scott. He couldn't stop laughing. Oh God, how ridiculous. This was NOT sexy. I started to laugh too.

Enough was enough. I yanked the rest of the receipt out, waved it a little in the air like I meant for it to be a prop, and then crumbled it up and threw it in the corner. I couldn't use the coupons anyway since they weren't even in English.

I was too tired to continue with the striptease, so we just moved along. Scott had no complaints and neither did I.

Early the next morning, Scott snuck back to his family's suite. Before he left my room, however, we decided to exchange numbers. He lived in Boston too although we made no promises nor did we set any expectations to see each other again. It was nice to have met him, period. I believed that sentiment was mutual.

Back in Boston, weeks turned into months and neither Scott nor I reached out to each other, and that was okay. He played a happy part in my journey of growth. For that, I am grateful.

# IAN LOVES IGUANAS

## IT WAS ALWAYS GOING TO END, BUT I
## DIDN'T SEE IT ENDING THAT WAY.

t was 4:00 a.m. on a Saturday morning in late spring when my alarm cut through the peaceful silence of my slumber. I immediately broke out in a cold sweat. Instead of being sound asleep like most people, I was about to roll out of bed and get ready for a 50K trail race taking place in a few hours.

Coffee was exactly what I needed to get my mind right. I sat on my couch for a few minutes with my cat enjoying the quiet as the caffeine slowly entered my bloodstream. In that moment, I couldn't remember why I signed up for the race or if it was a complete neurologic misfiring. Was it too late to just scratch? Probably. I made a mental note to not do this again.

Shit, the time! How could I already be running late? I needed to either get in the car immediately and drive the ninety minutes to the race or forget about it altogether. I threw the last of my items into my partially packed bag, grabbed more coffee, and ran to my car. I pulled into the parking lot of the race just in time to snag one of the last spots. I needed to get my race bib, use the restroom, assemble my gear, and then run to the start.

Race bib? Check.

Porta-potty? Gross, but check.

All my gear for thirty-plus miles in the woods? No check.

I looked at my watch and noted that I had exactly eight minutes to get to the race start a quarter mile away. I had none of my gear assembled.

Now, mind you, there were a sea of cars in the large parking lot and most well-prepared racers were leisurely making their way to the start line if they weren't already there. Except me. I decided to make use of the deserted parking lot to get ready. I took my bag out of my car and dumped all the contents on the ground. I stripped down to my short-shorts and sports bra. It was going to be a hot day and I wanted to be as naked as possible. Then I slathered on sunscreen, sprayed myself with bug spray, fixed my hair, and started to fill my hydration pack.

I noticed three gentlemen approaching me. Rather handsome fellows, I thought immediately. Too bad I looked like a lunatic or spaz, or both, sitting there in the middle of the parking lot with a giant mess around me. Maybe they wouldn't notice me even though they seemed to be heading directly toward me? Maybe I could just pretend to not see them?

Damn it, what was going on with this hydration pack? I couldn't seem to get it to close without water mix dripping out all over the place. I couldn't run thirty miles without it working.

"Hey there," said the bearded one from the gaggle of men. He was now standing directly above me.

"Hey there," I replied in a mostly irritated leave-me-alone kinda voice. Clearly this was not the time for small talk. I avoided eye contact, but it didn't help. It seemed this one guy wanted to continue to engage with me.

"We are parked next to you, and it seems you're blocking us from getting into the car," he says.

"Oh no, I'm so sorry. Let me get out of your way!" I began collecting all my crap and the bearded man started to laugh. What on earth was so funny?

I finally made eye contact. He was looking at me and smiling. "I'm just messing with you. We can get around all your stuff no problem."

"Okay, great," I say, now completely annoyed that I've lost twenty valuable seconds and I still couldn't figure out what was going on with the hydration pack. I returned to the task at hand and from the corner of my eye I see that this guy was still lurking around. Shouldn't he and his buddies be at the start line already?

"Do you run many of these 50K races?" he asks, hovering dangerously close to the hood of my car. Come on, guy. Seriously? What was it about this moment that said I wanted to be hit on?

I looked at him. Okay, he was good looking. Maybe in his early forties. Fit and probably a pretty fast runner too. I supposed I could fiddle with a hydration pack while making small talk for a minute.

We chatted just a little. But enough was enough. I still couldn't get the damn thing closed right and time had officially run out. I wished him good luck in the race, locked my car, and strapped on my leaky hydration pack. Off I went in an easy jog across the parking lot toward the start line.

*Swoosh, swoosh, swoosh.* That didn't sound good. Oh no, the pack was still leaking and now it was dripping down my back and onto my shorts. I had to stop and fix it once and for all.

Thinking I was far out of sight of the man-gaggle, I sat down and took off my gear. My water mix was all over the ground, making a giant puddle around me. *WTF is going on here?* I think. I couldn't start the race looking like I peed my pants and smelling like sweet electrolytes! I will be laughed at by humans and chased by bees.

I heard footsteps approaching and looked up.

Goddamn it! The gaggle of men were back. How the hell did they find me over here?

One of them said, "Oh man, that doesn't look good. You can't run a race if you don't have any water." No shit, Sherlock.

I don't remember what I mumbled in my moment of despair and frustration, but what I did notice, however, was that they didn't offer to help. Not a one of them. All three just stood there, towering over me, shaking their heads while smirking. Didn't they notice I was a damsel in distress? Why didn't they offer to help me rather than stare and make it worse?

Nada.

Finally, they left me alone. I literally couldn't fiddle with this thing any longer and following at a safe distance behind them, I made my way to the start line, leaving a trail of sugary water in my path.

The gun went off and we all dashed into the woods, with me at the back of the pack. I succumbed to the fact that my hydration pack was broken and would leave me dehydrated. On the positive side, the sweet orange mix that had completely drenched my lower body and clothes would help mask the scent of body odor and wash away any trail dirt.

At the first aid station a few miles in, I recognized that I would need to refill my nearly empty pack. Then, somehow, I finally figured out what was wrong this whole time. Okay, it was clearly user error. The washer thing around the lip was on incorrectly. Awesome! Maybe this day would turn around after all.

Fast forward a few hours. I was at mile 15, at the top of a steep climb, and about to make my way down this single track path. The course was a lollipop configuration, meaning you run out, make a loop in a single direction, then rejoin where you came from, retracing your steps back to the start line where you will finish. The stick of the lollipop was at mile 15. One of the lead racers had already passed me. I was moving very slowly.

Usually in trail ultramarathons, you run the flat portions, down-hills, and some of the moderate climbs. You then recover by walking the steep climbs. By the time I reached the woods, I realized that I was all by myself and decided to recover a bit longer by walking downhill.

As I was walking down the hill, a runner was coming up it. He looked familiar. Was he one of the gaggle-men? I couldn't be sure. I had avoided eye contact and was fully immersed in my water situation earlier that I probably wouldn't have been able to pick any of them out of a lineup.

This guy was running up the steep hill that I was attempting to walk down! This was nuts. I think that he must be a super athlete. So that he didn't notice that I was walking, I started to jog.

He sees me, smiles, and says, "Great to see you again!" and gives me a high five. Which one of the gaggle-men was this, I wondered?

I laughed to myself . . . maybe the sweet, orange electrolyte mix I had dumped all over the place attracted more men than bees? I wouldn't have been surprised if one of them, not that I could tell them apart, left a note on my windshield.

Hours go by. Somehow, I managed to get through.

Finally, the finish line was within sight. I was completely exhausted and sweaty. I was still able to walk, which seemed like a miracle.

Off in the distance I was able to see my car and noticed that the gaggle's car was no longer parked next to mine. *Aw, what a shame,* I think. I was now in the mind space to flirt and I had missed my chance.

Wait a second . . . what was that white thing on my windshield? Ha! I laughed out loud. It was a note. I opened it and in chicken scratch handwriting I read:

*"I met you before the race start. I hope you had a good race and enough water. – Ian <phone number>."*

How you like dem apples! This was awesome. I decided to text him later. Right then, all I wanted to do was get back to Beantown, shower, and consume unnecessary calories before the sun set.

Later that evening, I was on my roof deck with a couple of friends. I told them about the race and pulled Ian's note out of my pocket. They urged me to text him, but I had a better idea.

I was going to call.

His phone rang and a deep voice answered, "Hello?"

"Hey there, Ian. This is Christie. I got your note on my windshield from the race today."

"Oh, great! Thanks for giving me a call, Christie. How was your race?" he asked.

"Pretty good, thanks. I hope you had a solid race too. Look, I appreciate you leaving your number on my windshield but I'm not calling you for the reason you might expect."

There was an awkward silence from Ian. "Really? Why are you calling me?"

I almost felt bad, but I couldn't help myself in having a little fun. "So . . . unfortunately it seems that you or one of your friends dinged the whole side of my car today. It's a really big dent."

Now there was an even longer silence. "Oh no. Really? I am so sorry. Are you sure?"

"Yes, I am most definitely sure."

"Okay. Um, hold on one second, I'm here with my friends right now." Ian put his phone down and asked his buddies if someone dinged my car. There were some mumblings before he returned.

"Wow, so we don't think we dinged your car, but we are really sorry that it happened. Are you absolutely sure it was us?"

It was my turn for an awkward silent moment. I wanted to make him sweat for a few more seconds. Okay, that's enough. "Nah, I'm just messing with you! That's what you and your buddies get for hovering over me and not offering to help a lady in hydration pack distress."

He started laughing. "Guys, she was totally joking." I heard them all laughing. Good, I thought I was funny and now apparently this guy thought so too. "You are awesome. That was incredible." Poor guy sounded relieved, but his voice was quivering just a little bit. Hook, line, sinker.

I learned that Ian lived over an hour away from Boston but was in the area often. We agreed to meet up in the next week or two.

Over the next few months, I saw Ian every few weeks. Turned out he was not in his forties. His beard made him look older but in fact he was younger than me. He appeared to be very mature. He owned a home, had a solid job, and seemed to know what he wanted to do with his life. As we got to know each other, I realized that we had a good amount in common and conversation was easy. However, I was just not feeling the level of connection that I wanted. I realized that this fling was not going to last. I was a bit saddened by this. I had finally met an emotionally available and put together man, and outside of a dating app no less. This had all the signs of being something at the start.

Labor Day weekend arrived, and I was spending the first two days dog sitting for a friend. It was a bit depressing, to be honest. How did I not have any exciting plans for the official end of summer?

As if the universe heard me ask that question, Ian texted me. He was in town for the weekend and wanted to meet up. I was thankful to be dog sitting because it was a good excuse to not have him come over or stay with me. We weren't seriously dating and I craved my own space. But it would be nice to get out for a bit. We decided to meet up for lunch.

While out, Ian mentioned that the friend who drove him into Boston had changed plans and wasn't able to drive him back home, stranding him. Ian needed a ride back the next day. Shoot, he already knew that I would be done dog sitting with no other plans tomorrow. I had a premonition that he was going to ask me to give him a ride.

Unsurprisingly, he did ask, but also offered to make it worth my while. His parents lived in a really cool location along the water in Newport, Rhode Island, that fed out into the ocean. We could spend the day kayaking, hitting the beach, and grabbing some food. That sounded like a nice end to summer and I agreed to join him.

In fact, the day was a lot of fun. He was a gentleman and good company. We kayaked for at least five miles, stopping at a beautiful beach that was hopping with boaters and beachgoers. I had never been to this area before and I appreciated this new experience. It was beautiful and I found myself grateful for saying yes to the universe. Ian took me to a fantastic vegan restaurant and I ate my weight in food. All in all, it was a great end to summer.

It was now time to drop Ian off at home, but a storm was brewing. Literally, but in hindsight it could have been figuratively. It was a bit of a drive to his place and halfway there we found ourselves in the middle of a torrential downpour.

As I pulled up to his house I announced that I was going to grab my change of clothes, secretly thinking that this day had gone very well and perhaps might end even better. It would be nice to wait out the storm with some good company.

Ian led me up the stairs to his top level home and into the kitchen.

I stopped dead in my tracks. I wondered, *What the hell was going on here*? This was not what I was expecting. The kitchen was an absolute disaster. There was stuff everywhere. I mean, everywhere. I was repulsed. He ate food out of a kitchen that looked like that? It was a disease waiting to happen! And had he left all this food out while he was gone for the whole weekend? It wasn't making sense.

Directly off the kitchen was his bedroom . . . bow chica wow wow. Yeah, no. The bedroom was almost worse than the kitchen. There were stacked mattresses on the floor, a partially made bed, and a pillow not even in a pillowcase. It was all kinda gross. The only actual piece of furniture in his room was a makeshift bookshelf. After getting a full rundown of all the knick-knacks on his shelves, I decided that his chances of getting lucky were slim to none. I still wanted to drive home to Boston in comfort so I asked if I could use the bathroom to change into fresh clothes.

Ian said, "Sure thing. It's right around the corner, but I believe my roommate may be in there."

Things were starting to make sense. Okay, he had a roommate, which explained why the food had been left out in the kitchen. I wasn't completely grossed out, just mostly grossed out. However, I was completely turned off. I don't consider myself an elitist, but I was pushing forty and too old for a roommate, and I wasn't looking to date someone with one. There's no privacy in a relationship like that. It doesn't quite feel like an adult relationship. It's a dealbreaker.

Ian was right. His roommate was in the bathroom. Turned out, his roommate had a roommate. That was just too many people touching the grossness left out in the kitchen.

Deep in internal dialogue, I asked myself, *Do I wait for the bathroom to open up so I can change and go home? Or do I just make a run for it and head home, wet bathing suit and all, in the middle of a torrential downpour?*

As I was pondering this very important question, still standing in Ian's bedroom, I see a lovely hand-painted sign hanging on a door.

It reads, "Ian Loves Iguanas."

"Oh, that's nice. What is this about?" I asked.

Ian got very excited. "My mom made that for me! Do you want to see?"

"What do you mean, do I want to see? I see it now. I am looking at it." I was utterly confused.

Ian walked over to the door. "No, see what is *behind* the door."

I didn't really have a choice. He opened the door without waiting for a response.

And there it was. The world's largest iguana was sitting in the bathtub staring back at me. It was huge. It was scary. It looked angry. Why was it looking at me all angry? I hadn't opened the door. I hadn't put it in the tub. Had we woken it up from a nap or something? No one moved or blinked.

Was this humane? I found myself feeling sorry for this reptile, regardless of how unlovable it seemed.

Does an iguana count as a third roommate?

The iguana's name was Sheila. Still frozen in shock, I barely heard what he said. It's a girl. Okay, got it. I found myself wishing he hadn't opened the door. I was still processing the kitchen, the bedroom, the roommate, and the roommate's roommate. This was pushing me over the edge.

Eventually, I managed to pull my eyes away from the iguana's terrifying gaze and look around the bathroom.

It was most definitely a ninety-year-old grandma's bathroom. It was lined with pink tile from the late 1970s, and practically falling off the walls, coupled with the most outdated and grossest sink, floors, mirror, and decor. I found myself feeling bad that THIS is what the poor iguana had to look at for its entire life. Couldn't he have gotten some nice wallpaper? Maybe some ambient noise to help her reminisce about her young, wild, and free days in a tropical environment somewhere? No wonder she had resting bitch face. It was hating life! I would too.

Ian loved iguanas. But I don't think this iguana loved Ian.

Saved by noise coming from another room, I heard his roommate or his roommate's roommate exit the other bathroom. I made a run for it. I didn't say goodbye to Sheila, I just grabbed my bag and ran into the other bathroom, checking the bathtub immediately and pleased to see no other reptiles. This bathroom looked somewhat clean but I was not changing clothes. There was literally no time to spare. I needed to get the hell out of dodge before I either got a staph infection from touching anything, a concussion from a rickety bookshelf falling on my head, a hospital visit from an angry iguana bite, or possibly all of the above.

I peed.

I gave Ian a quick hug goodbye.

I left.

And with that, the summer, and this relationship, had come to an official end.

# ELEVEN DATES, ELEVEN POEMS

**YOU CAN'T FORCE LOVE EVEN IF YOU CHANNEL SHAKESPEARE HIMSELF.**

met him in the spring. I can't remember which dating app I saw him on, but I do remember he had a nice profile and seemed down to earth. Dark hair, a beard, and pretty hazel eyes. Hazel Eyes was clearly smart, had a solid job, and seemed to prioritize his health, all of which I found attractive. He lived in the suburbs though I had just recently moved from the suburbs to the South End of Boston. After a little banter back and forth, we decided to meet up for brunch one lazy Sunday morning in the Seaport District.

It was quiet that morning on the streets of Boston. So quiet, in fact, that the restaurant Hazel Eyes had picked for us wasn't even open. I arrived first, wondering perhaps if I was even at the right place. Off in the distance, I saw someone who looked like Hazel Eyes walking toward me on the otherwise empty street.

When he finally reached me, I could tell that Hazel Eyes was a little embarrassed that the restaurant was closed. He apologized multiple times, but I assured him it wasn't a big deal at all. We decided to walk around until we found someplace that was.

It was a nice walk and the conversation was easy. We had a lot in common. I liked his smile and his eyes, obviously. He was a year older than me, was divorced, and had a young daughter.

As a side note, I have never found having kids or being divorced to be a deal breaker unlike most women my age. Should I expect an almost middle-aged man to have not had a life prior to meeting me? There is a certain level of maturity I have seen especially among men who have at least one kid.

On the other hand, divorced men are a complete mixed bag. They are either sure of what it is they want because they have already experienced what it is they don't want, which I can relate to, or they have not yet processed their baggage and carry a great deal of festering emotional pain from their previous relationship. I have learned the hard way that you need to steer clear of the latter. An underripe avocado, for sure.

However, Hazel Eyes seemed emotionally available and ready for a real connection. I found this to be both a relief and an attractive characteristic.

Regardless, there was still something missing. I couldn't quite put my finger on the intangible aspect of a connection that I just didn't feel with Hazel Eyes.

Many of my girlfriends have told me that I jump to conclusions about the compatibility of a new date way too quickly. Perhaps my early dismissal of Hazel Eyes seems superficial and avoidant, and many of my friends would probably tell me that. I have been told that

I should not be so hasty deciding if there is long-term potential or not. I have gotten into arguments with friends and family about this.

I may or may not have all my critical faculties in place—I'll leave that to a professional to determine—but I do know that I have yet to be wrong about my assessments of the intangibles of a connection. This intuition has become second nature to me, and I have learned to trust it, for better or for worse.

The *second* I meet someone, I know if there will be a romantic connection or not. No, truly, I mean it. Anybody can look a certain way in a picture or dating profile, but when I see them in person, I just know.

Let's be clear, it has absolutely nothing to do with how attractive they are. It is about their vibe, the intangibleness of their essence, which I characterize as their energy. Some call it a person's aura, but I can't see auras. It's something that I can only sense; something that I can't quite put my finger on. The immediate feeling I get happens automatically, unconsciously, and without fail.

There are three scenarios that may take place when I meet a potential romantic partner. The first is a warm or familiar feeling. When eye contact is made, I feel drawn to them, like a magnet. The second is a feeling of repulsion. That sounds awful, I know. It's the opposite of the first. I literally feel pushed away from them. Again, it doesn't matter how handsome they are. I have been repulsed by incredibly attractive men and I can only explain it coming from an energetic field I don't really understand. The final scenario is one of neutrality. I neither feel drawn to them or repulsed.

Who wants to just "be neutral" with a potential romantic partner? No one. No one wants to be repulsed either. Don't we all want to feel a strong connection with our person? To be drawn to them on a physical, emotional, intellectual, and even spiritual level? I know I certainly do. I have felt that way and know it is possible. I also know it can be mutual. I want to that feel again.

Therefore, a feeling of neutrality is not much better than repulsion if I am looking for "The One." Perhaps dating a neutral connection for a while is possible, but I know it won't go anywhere long-term. Try explaining that to a friend who believes in "the slow burn" and letting things develop over time.

"The slow burn will last longer," they tell me. "A big spark turning into a big fire will just burn out quickly."

Well, that's just silly! I am a few decades removed from my Girl Scout days, but a slow burn may never become a big fire. Sometimes a slow burning candle is nothing more than its tiny little flame. I suppose that candle could catch fire to the curtains and before you know it, the whole place suddenly goes up in flames. What I do know, however, is a slow burn has never turned into a five-alarm fire in my dating life.

On the other hand, a giant bonfire fueled by a gallon of gasoline will have big flames and keep people warm. Even if it doesn't burn for a long time, it will still be smoldering long after the candle has burned out.

If I'm looking for true, long-lasting love, then don't I want to find the spark that ignites a bonfire rather than a candle? It seems obvious to me. Yet I'm still single so who the hell knows.

You may have been wondering what my initial sense was when I met Hazel Eyes. When he was about ten feet away from me, as he first approached, I pretty much felt nothing. I didn't feel warm, and I didn't feel repulsed either. I was just neutral. When I recognized this feeling, or lack thereof, I also felt just a tiny bit disappointed. I genuinely go into each first date hoping to feel that spark. Ninety-nine percent of the time I don't.

I also feel a little bad for my dates, in this case Hazel Eyes, because the poor guy can't read what is going on in my crazy little head. He didn't know that I had already written off a future with him before we even said hello or sat down. Unless he was cray-cray like me, he was still assessing me in a hopeful and open-minded way for the rest of the date and likely a few more.

Nonetheless, I was present, and I pride myself on treating all my dates with kindness and respect even if I will never see them again. Hazel Eyes and I had good conversation. I did enjoy his company. It was possible that the initial neutral feeling that I had from him may have lent itself to a casual dating scenario. In the back of my mind, I heard the voices of all those girlfriends who had told me to try the slow burn. I thought, what the heck, maybe I should try it. What do I have to lose?

At the end of the date, Hazel Eyes just looked at me as we said goodbye. I could tell he wanted to kiss me, but he didn't. He said he wanted to see me again and I agreed in an attempt to be the open-minded person my friends tell me I am not.

And so I began dating Hazel Eyes in The Slow Burn Experiment.

Although we were dating, we weren't exclusive . . . well, I certainly wasn't anyway. From my point of view, we developed a friendship first and foremost. He was an incredibly kind person that treated me with nothing but kindness and respect. By all objective means, he was exactly the kind of person someone would want.

For The Slow Burn Experiment, he was the ideal candidate to put on the figurative hamster wheel. I would continue to date him and see if a mutual connection caught fire.

A few weeks into seeing each other, I noticed how he looked at me. A subtle look that indicated, without a doubt, that he had feelings for me. Very likely more feelings than I had for him. I couldn't help but feel bad.

If I had made a promise to myself and the universe to try to treat everyone I dated with respect, then shouldn't I have tried to not let this poor guy develop more feelings for me if I was not moving along the same trajectory?

I decided that The Slow Burn Experiment wasn't working. I needed to let Hazel Eyes know that I didn't want to be in a long-term relationship with him. I am fairly certain that I didn't word it awkwardly like that, but honestly, I can't remember what I said. It was an uncomfortable conversation but one that I felt needed to be had.

He told me that he understood and asked me what I was looking for if not a long-term relationship. I clarified that I *was* looking for a serious partner, but that I just didn't feel it was him. I tried my darndest to sincerely let him know that I thought he was a tremendous human being and there was absolutely nothing wrong with him.

At the time, I thought he understood and believed me. With that understanding, he said he was open to continuing to see each other. He was, after all, a wonderful person and we got along very well. We had a lot in common and he treated me well. I thought that perhaps if I made sure I didn't lead him on, he wouldn't develop anymore feelings for me and he wouldn't get hurt. Isn't this what casual dating is all about?

With the cat out of the bag, we continued to date. A few weeks later, I noticed how he was looking at me again. Didn't we agree this would just be casual? I didn't lead him on, did I?

I had to revisit with Hazel Eyes that I was not looking for a long-term relationship with him. I knew, but didn't tell him explicitly, that the connection scale hadn't registered any higher on my end. My feelings were still in the neutral zone. Not even lukewarm, sadly. We had the same conversation and I reiterated the same points. He said he understood and promised not to get attached.

As far as I was concerned, The Slow Burn Experiment had proven to be a failure and I gave up on it. At this point, I just decided to focus on enjoying his company and continued to accept first dates with other men in my never-ending search for a bonfire spark.

Date number ten with Hazel Eyes took place going into week five. He mentioned, nonchalantly, that he liked to write poems as a way to make sense of his emotions and thoughts. We talked about it for a few minutes when he mentioned that he wrote a poem about me.

My big eyes got bigger, with a macroexpression of fear mixed with nervousness. I asked why he wrote a poem about me.

He said that he didn't want to scare me, but he thought I was a wonderful person and he wanted to put his feelings on paper. He assured me it was nothing for me to be concerned about. Again, we had the conversation, about my position on having a relationship with him. He seemed to still understand.

During week six and date eleven, Hazel Eyes offered to run a half marathon with me, which was nice but not necessary. I decided to take him up on it given our common interests and friendship built on mutual respect. He supported me as I attempted to get back in shape after my major surgery and I appreciated it.

On this date, he brought the poem he had written about me.

It was printed on thick stock paper, and it was obvious he put a lot of thought into it. I told him how flattered I was and that I would love to read it, which I would do after the race. Somewhere in my little pea-pickin' brain, I already knew what it would say, and I didn't want to deal with this before a race.

When I finally read the poem in front of Hazel Eyes, I wasn't surprised in the least to find that it was a love letter. He quite clearly had very strong feelings for me, if not feelings of love. It was sad to read, honestly. To know that someone feels a certain way about you but those feelings are not returned is awful. Really makes you feel like shit.

But, damn it! I didn't do anything wrong here, did I? I told him from the get-go that it was not going to lead anywhere. He told me repeatedly that he understood.

I sat him down and we began a long and painful, but respectful, two-hour conversation. It seemed to take forever to end things; an ending that perhaps neither of us had expected so soon. I felt bad. He was upset and I felt guilty, although deep down I knew I shouldn't have any feelings of guilt.

He finally left and headed back to the suburbs. A few hours later, he sent a long email saying that he thought I was afraid of commitment and that he and I were perfect for each other. He acknowledged everything I told him regarding my feelings, yet believed otherwise. There was no way, in his mind, that I couldn't grow feelings about him the same as he felt for me.

There was an attachment to the email. A zip file titled "Christiana" that included other poems he had written.

WHAT? More poems?! He made it sound like there had been only one.

I hesitated opening the file, afraid of what I might find. There were a total of eleven poems of varying lengths and topics, all about me.

I thought back on the number of dates we had and realized that we had exactly eleven dates. Was this a coincidence?

I decided to do what I thought was right and respond to his email because it was clear that he had been in a very vulnerable place. I told him, again, that I thought he was a wonderful person and called out all his amazing qualities. I told him that I appreciated how he felt about me but it wasn't mutual and would never be. I went so far as to say that he wasn't the one for me and that a better fit was out there waiting for him. That he would find her and it would be worth it. I didn't want him holding on to any hope for us. That, to me, would be cruel.

As months passed, I thought about him occasionally and wondered if he had moved on and found his person that he deserved. As harsh as it sounds, however, I did not miss him.

Six months later he sent me another email. He said that he thought of me often and missed me. He had wanted to send additional poems that he had written about me but hadn't. I think he wanted me to ask him to send these poems, but I didn't. I didn't want to read them. What I wanted was for him to let me go so he could find happiness with someone else, the person he was meant to be with, not me, which I kindly told him in response.

For me, this was like a punch in the gut from the universe. I had been that person, just like Hazel Eyes, trying desperately to convince someone, that I thought had mutually strong feelings toward me, that there was still something to explore. The difference in my situation, I convinced myself, was that I had confirmation of mutual feelings in at least one of my situations. I believed it was mutual, but it hadn't worked out for other reasons.

I found myself confused about my theories on connections in general, which I had so confidently believed until that moment. Was the universe telling me that I was wrong? That when I felt a connection it was not mutual perhaps, as it was with Hazel Eyes? Or was the universe delivering to me some sort of karma? I don't know and I probably won't be able to figure it out without hiring a world-renowned psychic.

What I do know, however, is that The Slow Burn Experiment was a failure on many fronts. Not only did I not get a different result, but I also feel that I hurt someone in the process. I don't like that. And, quite frankly, I don't like other people telling me how I should or should not feel about "The One."

I am a Scorpio—passionate, intense, stubborn. I know what I want, and I refuse to give up the search just because my eggs are shriveling while I continue to come up empty-handed. My fairy tale doesn't end with a lukewarm slow burn connection that may or may not ever turn into a bonfire. Damn it, I'm a pyromaniac and I want a bonfire to compete with Burning Man! That is how my fairy tale will end.

So, to all the people out there who want and believe in a slow burn . . . good for you! You do you, Boo-Boo.

Meanwhile, I'm gonna do me, unapologetically.

# MY FIRST SECOND FIRST DATE

**FEEL FREE TO REREAD THE TITLE UNTIL IT MAKES SENSE.**

"Swiping with intent" is a phrase I made up to characterize how and why I am on dating apps. If you don't intend to actually go on dates, then why are you wasting your time on a dating app?

In 2019, I had become a self-proclaimed expert in swiping with intent across state lines, specifically while visiting my sister in Virginia. On one particular visit, I swiped right on a handsome guy from Arlington. His name was Alex. He was clearly a swiper with intent as well, lining up dates without wasting any time. It was refreshing to connect with a no-nonsense dater who wasn't looking for a pen pal.

Alex also didn't waste any time sharing intimate details about himself up-front. On my profile he saw that I was open to having kids, however, he had no plans for any of his own. He went so far as to get a vasectomy and was open enough to share this factoid with me.

Alex asked if his vasectomy was a deal breaker for me, in which I replied that it was not. I was more concerned about meeting the right person than when, or if, I ever procreate. If I was focused on having a kid, what was keeping me from doing that right then? Nothing. I was a modern woman with the financial means to make it happen. It was a conscious effort on my part to seek out my forever person first and foremost rather than a baby daddy. Besides, vasectomies are technically reversible so who's to say he wouldn't change his mind after meeting *all this*.

To be honest, which I am at least 28 percent of the time, I would definitely like to have kids one day. I didn't think Alex needed to know that there was a chance that his "no kid" policy was a deal breaker before we even had the opportunity to meet. I wanted to be an open person and meet the guy for some coffee before I judged long-term potential.

Alex gave me his phone number so we could coordinate logistics more easily. I stored him in my phone as "Alex—VA Vasectomy" so I could easily remember who he was. Having been on what felt like a million dates in a few different cities, remembering each guy was becoming tricky.

The next day we met up for a late morning coffee at Northside Social, a popular first date spot in Arlington. Its location, on a corner of a busy intersection in the neighborhood of Clarendon, has lots of outdoor seating for swipers with intent meeting up for the first time.

After the usual greetings, he treated me to a mocha. We sat down and proceeded to talk for about forty-five minutes. It was a great conversation—easy, enjoyable—and turns out we had lots in common. I could definitely see myself going out with Alex again when in Virginia.

Alex seemed a little smitten with me. He said that he was bummed that I lived in Boston and would really love to see me again. "Do you have any interest in talking on FaceTime while you're back in Boston?" he asked. Oh God, no. That's too much of a commitment after a forty-five minute first date! Couldn't we just casually meet up again when I was back in town?

I tap danced around the question a bit and decided to confirm my interest by suggesting we meet up in person in the next month or so, whenever I was back in the area. He seemed to accept this idea.

I returned to Boston and Alex —VA Vasectomy texted me every so often. Nothing remarkable took place during our conversations. For whatever reason, I returned to Virginia a couple of weeks later but decided not to reach out to him. I can't remember exactly why, but either I had other plans or just didn't feel like it. Alex was none the wiser.

As time went on, my intent to meet up again began to fade as I started to date someone else in the Virginia area. I started to kick the can down the road with Alex, hoping maybe he would forget I existed, and I wouldn't hear from him again.

One day while at a work event he texted me. It was more of a "sext" actually. He wanted me to talk dirty to him, which I was definitely not into. Rather than get offended, I was strangely happy. YES. This was how I could politely exit out of the situation and relieve myself of the self-imposed obligation of meeting up again. My interest had waned to a nonexistent level and I needed to be released from the match. Poor guy.

I responded, telling him that I don't engage in sexting, especially after only a forty-five-minute coffee date. Perhaps we were not meant to be. I said I was sorry, but I had to let this match go to the wayside. Alex apologized and asked for a second chance. I said no hard feelings, but it had run its course. Time to part ways. Bye-bye,

Alex—VA Vasectomy.

Fast forward to spring 2021. I had moved from Boston to Virginia and I was swiping left and right so much that I almost developed carpal tunnel syndrome. I didn't live in Arlington, but was in the area regularly so I was able to swipe on the locals there and in my own town. I was essentially swiping on all of Northern Virginia, DC, and even into Maryland at times. There were lots of fish in this sea and my social calendar was packed like a can of sardines!

One handsome man came across my queue. Oh, looky-looky. Nice eyes, nice smile, seemingly fit. He looked vaguely familiar but I couldn't quite place him. We matched. His name was Alex. We lined up a date pretty quickly—coffee that Sunday morning somewhere in Arlington.

Prior to the date, Alex mentioned via the dating app that he had had a vasectomy. He wanted to know if that would be a deal breaker. Now, mind you, I had completely forgotten about Alex—VA Vasectomy. His number had been long deleted from my phone and I had been on no less than a hundred first dates since the one with him a couple years ago. I know you already know where this is going, but can you please humor me and pretend, for a moment, to be surprised at the ending?

No, I tell him, a vasectomy wouldn't be a deal breaker. I thought to myself, *Vasectomies are reversible and who's to say he doesn't want to procreate when he sees* all this? (Side note: at least my internal dialogue is consistent!)

I started to think at this point that I vaguely remember him. I wondered if this was Alex—VA Vasectomy. Hmm, maybe. I really didn't know. I had been on so many first dates. Was it bad that I literally couldn't remember names or faces? Maybe.

We decided to meet at Northside Social for coffee. Now I was thinking, this had to be the same guy, right? What were the chances that a guy with the same name and backstory would choose the same first date spot?

Northside Social was the unofficial first date spot in the area, where hundreds of desperate souls got highly caffeinated each and every day. Perhaps it was a strange coincidence he chose this place. Either way, I knew I'd be sure once seeing him.

I stood outside Northside Social at date time waiting for Alex. It was a warm, sunny day and I reflected on the number of people there sipping coffee and seeking love.

I watched as Alex approached. *Was he Alex — VA Vasectomy,* I asked myself? As he got closer, I still couldn't tell. I really wasn't sure. How was it that I didn't know if it was the same guy? We had such a nice date the first time. Shouldn't I at least have remembered his face? Yet my memory failed me.

Alex approached and gave me a friendly greeting. He commented at the large crowd of people gathered at our date spot and suggested that we go across the street to a diner where there were no lines. As we walked over, I asked Alex if I looked familiar to him because I thought we may have gone out on a date before.

He didn't think so and offered up a really nice compliment saying that if we had met before, there was no way he would have let me get away. I was flattered.

When we sat down in the diner and started talking, it was clear that we had a lot in common. Conversation was easy. I couldn't help myself and asked Alex again if he thought we had met up before. I then proceeded to tell him what I remembered about a first date some time ago with a guy with the same name who also had a vasectomy. He couldn't remember me and asked why we never went out again if we had in fact met before.

I said that we had kept in touch for a little bit after I went back to Boston, but it didn't go any further. He half smiled, looked at me and said, "Did I happen to say something inappropriate on text?"

I laughed with relief and said, "Why yes you did," and told him what happened. He apologized. I felt the need to be completely honest and said that I was actually not at all offended. I was not proud about it, but I had used it as an excuse to politely make my exit.

Alex confirmed what I had already known. We should both assume that the Alex from two years ago who had a vasectomy and talked dirty on text message with near strangers was in fact the same Alex in front of me.

I thanked him for at least taking me to a different place for our second date, even if it wasn't the original plan. It was both of our first second first dates. We had a good laugh about it.

Alex expressed interest in seeing me again. I found him to be good company and very attractive, but was more certain that I wanted to have kids eventually. His position had not changed. I didn't see this going anywhere long-term. We decided to leave the door open for something casual and ended the date.

Over the coming weeks, I was very busy with work, accepting new first dates, and prioritizing a couple others for second and third dates.

History was bound to repeat itself, it seemed. After two first dates, it turned out that Alex didn't make the cut.

Well, actually, he did make *The Cut*, if you know what I mean, but unfortunately not the one in my dating life.

# DOWN BY THE RIVER

## LOVE IN THE TIME OF CORONA IS A STRANGE THING INDEED.

n late spring 2020, COVID was in full swing. I was still living in Boston at the time and my favorite part of the year was finally arriving. The weather was turning gorgeous but the whole city was still mostly shut down because of the pandemic.

Those of us who were living on the edge and keeping up our dating were probably doing so with a great deal of caution. Dating for me evolved during this time so I could, as safely as possible, meet people. It was a must. My ovaries were shriveling up and my eggs getting scrambled with each passing day. I was not going to let the pandemic keep me from meeting Mr. Right, or so I thought.

The apps certainly never turned off during the pandemic. I found many people on dating apps with zero intent to go on actual dates. I remember one guy who swiped on me first, asking after we matched, if I was going on dates. I said yes, to which he responded, "We do not share the same values." Perhaps I have a simplistic mindset, but if you're on a dating app, it's because you want to GO ON A DATE.

Whatevs. I still can't figure out why that guy, and several others, wanted to waste everyone's time if they just wanted a pen pal. You're better off finding someone in a prison cell. That's a safe way to communicate without getting COVID.

Anyway, I like to find the positive and opportunities within even the most unpleasant of situations. Love in the time of Corona was no different. Most of life's enjoyment is all about perspective, is it not?

With bars and restaurants closed, there was no "grabbing a drink" or a "quick bite to eat" on a first date that was never actually quick. Pre-pandemic, dates always had the risk of dragging on and on. It's awkward at times to end a date early without hurting someone's feelings.

Then, in walked the pandemic. No more awkwardly long dates going nowhere other than down the drain, including time and money. No more unnecessary liquid calories that had to be run off the next morning. No more Ubering all over the place to meet up with someone new. No more picking out a cute first date outfit and prepping hair and makeup.

Now we had circumstances that coincided nicely with how I liked to spend my time anyway! Yes to going on a socially-distanced more or less walk around town for a first date. Yes to burning calories instead of consuming them. Yes to having to end a date when our legs get tired after about forty-five minutes. Yes to early bedtime. Yes to walking rather than throwing money into an Uber. Yes to wearing a face mask for the most part, thus reducing the need to put on any makeup whatsoever. Yes to wearing my work from home athleisure attire on a first date. Yes, yes, and yes again!

The pandemic dating scene's silver lining was looking more like platinum, and I was soaking up every bit of it.

Not everyone continued to date, obviously. To each their own.

Perhaps, due to the limited supply of people on the market, I met more than a handful of interesting guys that I may not have otherwise, one being David.

I can't remember his real first name, but I do remember he looked like a young David Duchovny, who played Fox Mulder in *The X-Files*. I was a huge fan of the show back in the day, especially the character Mulder. I used to walk around the house singing a popular song at the time, *"David Duchovny, why won't you love me?"* I was a rather pathetic tween now that I think about it.

One Friday, David and I matched on a dating app. His profile was quite unique. It was a mix of humor and humility, with some cool pictures sprinkled in for extra effect. One was of him standing in front of a partially visible van. He wrote that he was currently traveling around the country.

I'm a self-proclaimed "picture creeper." If you send me a picture, I will likely zoom in and check out what's going on in the background. I don't Google-stalk people I haven't met, like many of my friends tend to do. You can learn a lot about someone based on what they don't even realize is in their pictures.

I didn't find anything too unusual about David's pictures, other than the one with the van. From the picture, I couldn't tell what type it was, that is, was it your typical white pedophile van, a camper van, or a minivan? I had no idea given the angle of the shot. However, I did notice that behind him were blue LED lights on its ceiling, which was concerning to say the least. I did my best to not judge him because I hadn't even met him yet.

David chatted me up right away. He was eager to meet me. I found him funny and personable. He also mentioned that he lived in his van. I laughed, thinking he was joking, but he wasn't. In hindsight, this is likely where most of David's first dates slip through his fingers. He asked if he could call me through the app and explain his choice of living quarters. I hesitated but agreed. What the heck. What's there to lose?

He explained a little about his backstory. Just before the pandemic hit, he decided to get a van and live a migratory lifestyle traveling across the United States. He started in Portland, Oregon, and meandered through all sorts of random places before landing in Boston just a few days prior.

After telling me about his travels, he asked me if we could meet up that night. Having already made plans with a friend to go for a walk, I declined. David pushed a bit, saying he was heading to New Hampshire the next morning and then heading home to see his mom next week. He really wanted to meet up with me that evening.

I didn't want to cancel plans with my good friend, not to mention that I was not looking for a serious relationship with a migratory van man. I suggested that we meet up the next time he *rolled* through town.

However, David convinced me to go for a walk with him after my friend walk date. He said he was looking for a reason to stay in one place. Maybe I was that reason, he joked.

Secretly, I was only thinking about going for another walk. SCORE! Double the caloric burn without a single penny spent! What else was I going to do that evening anyway? Laying in my hammock making out with my cat didn't make for an eventful evening.

With an agreement in place, I asked him where he was parked.

He said, I shit you not, "I'm down by the river."

I laughed out loud. What, were we in a *SNL* skit? Who says this?

David sounded serious. "No, really, I live down by the river. The Charles River. Ever heard of it?"

I laughed again. Yes, I had heard of the Charles River just like every New Yorker has heard of the Hudson River.

"Yes, David, I know where the Charles River is located. Where exactly are you parked?" I asked.

David seemed a bit confused on where exactly he was, but described what sounded like a parking lot by the Boston College crew dock. "Can you pick out where we will meet? I am mobile." I suppressed another laugh. "However, I do prefer a place with free parking."

OMG. What did I get myself into? This was either going to be a totally random yet fun date, or I was going to get abducted.

I picked the location that was most convenient to me, considering I was squeezing him into my existing walk schedule. Without him knowing where I lived, which was near the Whole Foods, I suggested meeting there. Free parking!

We agreed to meet at 7:00 p.m., which would allow enough time for a walk before it got dark, thus decreasing the chances of an uninvited abduction.

Right before we are about to meet up, a long line of millennial shoppers jammed up the parking lot and road leading to Whole Foods. There was no way David was going to find a spot. Knowing he didn't want to pay for parking, I grabbed a roll of quarters and found an open spot on the street across from my apartment. From the sidewalk, I could see my windows and almost make out the shape of my cat by one of them.

While I waited for David, I messaged him letting him know I found him a spot and provided him with directions. "Don't worry," I said, "I will pay for the parking." There went my streak of free dates. Looked like I was going to have to break the bank on this one.

I was standing on the corner, exactly where David was supposed to drive by, at seven o'clock on the dot. There were no vans. I thought that maybe he was lost.

I waited a few minutes before hearing a van approach. You read that correctly. I heard the van before seeing it. It made a low rumbling noise accompanied by a whole lot of clanking. Before looking up, I imagined the noise was coming from a small dump truck or perhaps a convertible dragging empty coffee cans with newlyweds inside.

Nope. I looked up to see a silver minivan driven by a man in his thirties, from the looks of it. I assumed this was my date. Unfortunately, he made a right at the intersection when he should have gone straight through and toward me. Fortunately, this gave me a chance to get a good look at the tenement on wheels.

The back bumper was practically falling off. That's what was clearly causing all the noise. However, even worse than the condition of the vehicle was the fact that it had Ohio plates!

Ohio drivers may be the absolute worst. Really. There's literally nowhere more dangerous in the world than driving through Ohio in a snowstorm. I am still scarred from a 2009 trip through The Buckeye State. Having lived in multiple states, I can personally attest to the fact (yes, a fact) that Ohio drivers put "Massholes" to shame.

It occurred to me that this was my chance to skip out. I could quickly blend into the Whole Foods crowd and chalk this almost-date up to being too open to what the universe offered me. I'm sure that my cat would be happy if I came in off the street. I glanced up at my window to see if she was going to tell me what to do. Sadly, she wasn't at the window anymore . . . perhaps she didn't want to watch this train wreck, I mean van wreck, unfold?

At that moment, I remembered that dating was as much about experiencing new things and learning as much about myself as I would learn about my date. Perspective, right? I decided that something good was likely to come out of a walk with a stranger. Besides, he probably needed a shakeout walk from sitting behind the wheel for so long.

I called David through the app and he confirmed that he was in that van heading in the wrong direction. I directed him back toward his reserved parking space. As he pulled into the spot, I quickly threw some quarters into the meter and slowly backed away ten feet so there was no chance of being yanked inside against my will. FYI, I was too far away to see if there were in fact blue LEDs inside.

David got out of the van with a giant smile on his face. Perhaps surprisingly, he was a very handsome and fit guy. He immediately came off as friendly and down to earth. He cracked a joke or two, so I figured we would have good conversation on our walk. That surprised me. I was reminded, again, that I shouldn't be so quick to judge. He thanked me for the seventy-five cents that I threw in the meter and off we went on our walk through the South End and Back Bay.

Over the course of our two mile walk, David shared two stories in particular that still stand out in my memory.

The first was about how he got COVID several months prior, right at the onset of the pandemic. While making a pit stop in Austin, Texas, he had gone to a dance club to meet some new people and dance the tango, one of his passions.

He was convinced that his tango dancing experience was to blame. Apparently, it takes two to get COVID.

I asked him how bad he had it and he explained that it had been absolutely awful, but thankfully he was able to "rest at home."

I asked for clarification on what "resting at home" meant if he was from Portland but living in a van. Had he driven back to Portland? Had he gone to the hospital?

"No, no, it wasn't that bad," he said. He just stayed in his van. How someone can recover from a pretty bad bout with a deadly virus while living in a van by themselves was both terrifying and concerning. I expressed that I was glad he was okay, though didn't ask if he still went "tango dancing."

Not wanting to hear more details, I changed the subject to

something more pleasant, like food.

It seemed that David and I had similar food preferences: me, mostly vegan, and David, vegetarian. This made sense to me considering that living in a van was not conducive to storing and cooking meat. It's not like his minivan had room for a minifridge.

I asked him how he exactly stored and ate his food.

He said, "Interesting you ask me that. I do what I call a Car Bar, my version of a salad bar in my van."

"Please do tell," I respond. Shame on me for asking for details.

"So, what I do is keep a cooler in my van with some leafy greens, tomatoes, maybe a cucumber or two. Oh, and can't forget about the salad dressing. But since I don't use plates that often, I improvise with my mouth. First, I take a nice handful of spinach and shove it in my mouth."

David proceeded to tell the rest of his story, sounding as if he actually had a mouthful of spinach. We stopped walking for a moment so he could show me. He stood on the sidewalk with his head leaning slightly back, as if a spinach leaf would otherwise fall out. Please imagine this along with me.

"Then, I throw a cherry tomato or two in there. Perhaps I'm able to take a bite out of the cucumber. Occasionally I add broccoli to mix it up. As you can see, my mouth is full with all the necessary ingredients of a salad, minus the dressing."

At this point, I could barely understand what he was saying. David was in full mouth reenactment mode. "To add some favor to the mix, I grab the dressing, lean my head back like this. Then I squirt a good amount of dressing straight into my mouth. But I can't forget the best part, which is to swish it all around in my mouth so the salad gets tossed. Then, finally, I chew. Genius, right?"

I was speechless. I love a salad, but would never, ever want to witness this display with actual food. I responded with a benign comment like, "Wow, well you certainly know how to be creative."

David seemed pleased with my response and became excited. "I know, right? It's so weird though. Women have told me explicitly that my Car Bar is a deal breaker for them."

Pause here for a second. I was intrigued by this statement. What did he mean that his eating habits were a deal breaker for most women? Multiple thoughts went through my mind simultaneously.

First of all, what woman got *inside* the van to witness what and how he eats? I had been consciously focused on not getting pulled inside, so I was fascinated that a woman apparently would willingly get in.

Secondly, he said "women." That's plural for woman. *Multiple* women had ventured into the van to witness this?

And finally, perhaps I'm the weirdo here, but last time I checked, he lived in a van down by the river. Wasn't *that* the deal-breaker?

I was so confused. Thankfully, our walk was coming to an end. I thanked him for a lovely walk and wished him well on his trip to New Hampshire and beyond.

He asked me if we could stay in touch and I said sure, knowing that neither one of us was going to. Minus the visualizations I had during his story telling, he was a pleasant date, and I enjoyed his company. It was a decent use of my Friday evening hours. I bode him fair adieu and headed home to my cat.

Mind you, my home was literally across the street from the parked van, so I decided to take the scenic route. I wandered a couple blocks over before looping back around and entering the apartment out of sight. I didn't want him to know where I lived in case he decided to remain there all night. It was late enough that street parking was free until 8:00 a.m. the next morning.

A few hours later, I saw that David was still parked in the van outside of my building. Part of me felt bad and part didn't. Had he been so eager to have a date with me in hopes of coming to my apartment for some plated food, a shower, a bed, and maybe a bit of "tango dancing"? I don't know. I felt just a smidgen bad for even wondering that. Who's to say he was not completely happy just the way he was living his life?

Dating can be so unexpected, for good and bad. I applaud David's perspective on life and dating, and I like to think that he positively influenced shaping my own personal journey. I wouldn't be surprised if his openness to the universe and search for new experiences have led him to find his match and park his van once and for all.

# WHEN YOU LEAST EXPECT IT

## NOT BEING SOLO ON A SOLO TRIP.

The sun was about to set on Tamarindo Beach in Costa Rica. I was standing in its warm orange glow, a giant smile on my face, my feet sinking into the wet sand. I had just caught a wave, riding it to the shoreline. Mind you it was a very small wave, but a wave nonetheless.

I held my surfboard under my right arm. It was heavy, but I carried it proudly.

Surf Boy, who I met at the hotel earlier that morning, approached me with a big smile on his face. All six feet five inches of him hovered over me. He gave me a high five and then leaned down to lay one on me.

I had been too busy smiling off into the sunset to notice he was trying to kiss me. *Whoops*. Rather than let him kiss me on the lips, I intentionally moved my head in such a way that he missed and planted one on my left eye. Thank God I had been squinting into the sun, otherwise he would have gotten my actual eyeball.

How awkward. The poor guy had probably been waiting to kiss me for the better part of the day.

So the first kiss, after much anticipation on his part, fell flat . . . or should I say, fell onto my round eye.

You know when it's time for the first kiss and whether you want it or not. I wasn't really digging this dude in that way, unfortunately for him. There was nothing wrong with him, but he was just not my guy. After hanging out for a bit that day, I had become less and less interested in hooking up with him.

He inched his face closer to mine. *Oh God*, I thought, *he is clearly going to go for it again.*

Maybe my attempt to conceal awkwardness with obliviousness was being interpreted as legitimate interest. As he started to lean in for kiss number two, I quickly began to think about how we had gotten to this place.

I had arrived a few days prior in Guanacaste Province, Costa Rica, dedicated to a solid seven days of scuba diving. I deliberately arrived alone, craving solo time. Surf Boy arrived around the same time as me and was lodging at the same hotel. He was also in Costa Rica for some quality diving. We had met on the way to the boat that morning and it was certain that we would be on the same boat for the next two days of diving.

My new dive buddy was seemingly into me within a few minutes of meeting. I don't say that out of oversized ego. No, I say it because he literally told me that he was.

As we were waiting to get on the dive boat that morning, and a whopping forty-five minutes after meeting, he went so far to say how happy he was to have met me. That he hadn't expected to hit it off with someone and that I needed to come visit him in California some time.

I didn't really know what was going on and how our meeting had escalated so quickly. I very consciously tried not to lead this guy on since I hadn't yet decided how far I wanted to take it. I was on vacation after all and a free, modern woman. Single and ready to mingle, but not if I wasn't totally feeling it.

Over the course of the day, he told me that he used to be a surf instructor and would love to give me lessons. Of course, I wanted to take him up on the offer. I'm not stupid. I was in Costa Rica and could get free surfing lessons? Hell to the yeah.

After a day of diving, we headed down the coast to grab dinner. Then Surf Boy and I hit some waves before the sun set. To be clear, the waves hit me more than I did them. Although, I am proud to say that I was able to stand up a few times and not make a complete embarrassment of myself.

So, there I am, basking in the sunset after riding a full wave into shore when the wet lips of this guy I just met quickly approach my face.

I let him kiss me on my lips this time. Oh God, the kiss tasted like garlic.

I made it a quick kiss, pretending to be excited to go back in the water and catch another wave. As I ran back into the waves, I thanked my surf instructor for his excellent coaching.

I looked back at him. He was standing there with a goofy smile on his face, watching me paddling over a wave on a giant surfboard. I felt bad because he really seemed smitten with me.

The next day, our second day together on the boat, Surf Boy got somewhat handsy with me massaging my shoulders. I'm all for a free massage just like I love me some free surf lessons, but I really didn't want one in front of a group of people that I hardly knew. The day before I was single and now he was figuratively pissing all over me to mark his territory. That's what it felt like anyway. Since when did a couple of garlicky kisses make a relationship?

After a minute or two of the free public massage, I kindly leaned over and told Surf Boy very politely that PDA makes me uncomfortable. He said he understood and appreciated my directness. I was direct, but not exactly honest. I didn't want to partake in PDA from a guy I just met as if we were in some kind of relationship or madly in love after just one day.

He was intelligent, pretty good looking, clearly athletic, and had the financial means to hop on a plane for a week in paradise to pursue a hobby like scuba diving. Maybe it was the several year age gap between us or the different life stages we were in, but I just didn't find myself all that attracted to him.

He respected my wishes and refrained from PDA other than a few lingering lower back touches when he thought no one was watching. Again, not a bad guy, but he just wasn't picking up on the cues. I felt uneasy. I was either going to have to let this run its course painfully slowly, or smack it down with a hammer at some point.

Our destination that day was the Bat Islands, a group of islands known for diving with bull sharks. This was a stressful situation for me. I had only logged fourteen dives in total to date and was about to do a negative entry into the water while trying not to get eaten alive by the third deadliest shark on the planet.

I was nervous and not thinking about Mr. Love Bug sitting next to me. He, however, was thinking about *me*. As I tried to get myself in the right frame of mind for the dive, he was whispering in my ear about how sexy he found my New York accent. He purred that he hadn't expected to "vibe" so well with someone. I wasn't paying attention to him and mumbled "uh huh" and "yeah" every so often in response. I was focused on prepping my gear to make sure I didn't die in the waters off the Bat Islands and not garlicky sunset kisses on the beaches of Costa Rica.

Time to dive! With a deep breath to calm my nerves, I back rolled off the boat and descended toward the sea floor. I assumed a position above a group of rocks a few feet away from the divemaster, Surf Boy, and a couple from San Diego who I enjoyed getting to know that week.

I scanned the murky water looking for bull sharks, but instead of sharks, I see Surf Boy blowing me kisses through his regulator bubbles. He's not even looking for the sharks!

I think, *What the fuck, dude? Seriously? Bull sharks are lurking in the shadows, and you want to blow me kisses?* I ignored him. I was on a solo trip, damn it, and this had to be the least romantic thing that could happen with someone I was becoming less and less interested in.

I refocused on the task at hand and fully immersed myself in the experience. Several giant bull sharks circled around our group, a few even coming within ten feet of me. It was thrilling. And terrifying. And perhaps because it was both thrilling and terrifying, I was having the time of my life.

After fifty minutes under water and many bull shark sightings, we resurfaced, sharing our experiences with one another. Of everyone on the trip that day, I had seen the most sharks and at the closest distance. Then someone pointed out that my hand was covered in blood.

It seemed that I had gotten cut on the rocks while trying to stabilize myself in the strong underwater surge. Once we realized that it was not a serious injury despite all the blood, we all had a good laugh. No wonder I saw the most sharks, I had literally been shark bait!

As the divemaster bandaged me up, Surf Boy lurked close behind.

I just couldn't shake him. Even though we were on a tiny boat out in the middle of nowhere, I maneuvered through the rest of the divers to get away from him. Couldn't this guy take a hint? I almost died and I needed a moment to myself!

After eating some pineapple and Costa Rican cookies, and finally calming down, I was able to participate in the next dive before heading back to shore.

Back at the dock, Surf Boy asked me if I want to go surfing again with him, as this was his last night at the hotel. I couldn't think of anything else to do so I said yes. I know, I know. What was I thinking? Blame it on blood loss.

We headed back to Tamarindo Beach to catch some more waves. Well, I caught about four and spent the rest of the time watching him surf.

He joked with me about what he looks for in a relationship: the three "Ss." His dream girl was someone that he can scuba dive with, surf with, and have sex with.

With a twinkle in his eye, he said that he never did all three in one day.

Damn it, the guy was able to find the only possible way he could get to my heart, which was through my competitive streak.

I paused for a moment, deep in my own thoughts. He wasn't unattractive. Other than his breath, he was probably pretty good in bed. Did I want to go down in his record book as the one who met all three criteria?

*Maybe*, I think. The chance was remote, but there was a chance.

As the sun set, we left the beach and meandered around the town to find a place to eat. It was a beautiful evening in paradise and I had some time to make my decision before we headed back to the hotel.

Surf Boy ended up making my decision easy for me. We were standing outside a restaurant evaluating the menu when I asked him what I thought to be a legitimate question. He didn't seem to understand what I was asking, so I rephrased my question. He then made fun of me, and not in a flirty kind of way.

There was a superiority to it, which made me feel stupid. It didn't matter if my question was stupid or if I didn't formulate a nonstupid question in a nonstupid way in that moment. What mattered was that a guy that apparently had the hots for me and wanted to get in my pants was making fun of me.

Though infuriated, I kept cool, took a breath, and responded. I pretended that I found the answer myself on the menu and it was all good, when really it wasn't. I was proud of myself for not blowing up. I can be hot-headed from time to time.

The verdict had come in and Surf Boy's chance of achieving all three Ss in one day wasn't going to happen (with me anyway).

Like me on a surfboard, whatever tiny spark he thought existed between us was wiped out. I reminded myself that I was still on a solo vacation and just happened to have companionship for the evening. There were no commitments after all.

I tried to keep things civil as we had dinner and then made our way back to the hotel. Seeing the expectant look on his face back at the hotel lobby, I told Surf Boy that I was still on East Coast time and needed to get some rest. After all, fatigue and dehydration are major factors for decompression syndrome when scuba diving! Thank goodness for complicated hobbies that align well with my avoidant tendencies.

The following morning, I bumped into Surf Boy at breakfast and we bid each other a fond adieu before heading out for the day's activities: me diving and he the rain forest as his scuba excursions had come to an end. It was a pleasant goodbye and I appreciated having had company over the past few days. Nevertheless, I found myself looking forward to an afternoon without him.

The dive trip that day was a lot of fun. My favorite couple that I had met on earlier dive days was on the same boat with me again. It felt like a fresh new day and I felt unencumbered. I was able to be present in the moment and enjoy diving in an extraordinary place.

After the diving excursion, I took a nap on the hotel beach, enjoyed cocktails at the happy hour, had dinner, and retreated to my room to meditate and then sleep. It was quiet, uneventful, yet so fulfilling.

The next morning, feeling refreshed and rejuvenated, I arrived at the beach for another day of diving. Not only was my favorite couple going, but a new, and very handsome man, was joining our group it seemed.

He had dark hair that was cut short on the sides, an athletic build, and stunning blue eyes. I immediately found him incredibly attractive.

*Ah,* I think to myself, *this is what I'm talking about*. The dynamic with Surf Boy had seemed so forced. If I'm going to have a fling with someone, I don't want to question whether or not I'm into them.

I was getting ahead of myself. I hadn't even met the guy. He could have been married, not into women, or quite frankly, not even interested in me. I reminded myself that it didn't matter because I was on a *solo* trip to scuba dive. Eye candy was welcomed but not needed. Either way, I hid behind my oversized reflective sunglasses, which allowed me to gawk in stealth mode.

Diving can expend a lot of energy so the Tupperware of Costa Rican cookies was my regular hangout spot on the boat during surface intervals. After the first dive, Blue Eyes made his way over to the cookie container where I offered him my unsolicited recommendations.

He found me funny; I found his laugh genuine. I insisted he report back post-consumption. I grabbed a cookie for myself and found a seat to park myself during the break. It seemed I had caught his attention. Blue Eyes grabbed a bottle of water and sat down next to me. We started chatting, covering the basics like what we did for a living, where we were from, how many dives we'd clocked. Turned out he was a brand new diver just like me. Surprisingly, we both said that scuba diving was our COVID hobby. I had an immediate kinship with this handsome guy.

However, much to my dismay, right in the middle of me throwing some mad game, a multimillionaire egomaniac on the boat interjects and Blue Eyes gets sucked into a conversation with him. It became so involved that I completely gave up. My flirt game had been hijacked.

Finally, Blue Eyes was able to pull himself away from the millionaire. He looked around the boat until he caught my attention. I knew by the look on his face that he felt the same about our interrupted conversation. I smiled and winked.

The second dive of the day was fun. I spied an octopus or two and pointed them out to everyone underwater, including Blue Eyes. I thought that maybe he'd be impressed with my scuba skills and keen eye for marine life.

Once back on the boat, I was curious to see if Blue Eyes would seek me out. Much to my joy, he found his way over and we started conversing again.

I learned he also was on a solo trip. And single. He had planned to explore Costa Rica for three weeks, but today was his only day of diving. I was saddened by this. Finally, someone I could really see myself getting to know and I wouldn't even have the chance.

I asked him what else he had planned for himself, and he listed all his many adventures. When I told him how jealous I was, he looked at me with those gorgeous eyes and said that maybe I should extend my trip. I laughed. I didn't know what he meant by that and I didn't want to read into it. I joked about how I had to go back to work, but since I worked remotely, perhaps I could upload a picture of my office as my virtual background and no one would know that I was actually deep in the Costa Rican rainforest rather than home in Virginia. He laughed and suggested I do that. How tempting, really.

*Damn it.* This guy was quite a catch and giving me signs of interest.

We talked the entire ride back to the dock. Blue Eyes wanted to know if I had plans for the rest of the day. I didn't have any and neither did he. Holding my breath, I wondered if he would ask me to join him for lunch and then go exploring.

He didn't, but the moment was not yet lost. Everyone was in the dive shop regrouping after the trip, when quite abruptly, Blue Eyes announced that he was heading out and wished us all a nice rest of the week. He pushed the door open and walked out.

The figurative door had been open to hang out, not to walk out quite literally!

My heart sank. *How had this catch slipped through my fingers?* The usual thoughts about what I may have done to mess it up ran through my head.

Then I started to think about Surf Boy and how he had thought all the signs were there. I had not been on the same page as him. Was this the universe's way of letting me know that just because I thought there was mutual interest with Blue Eyes that that wasn't really the case?

I went back to the hotel and grabbed a front-row seat along the nearly empty beach chairs. I should have reveled in my time alone, which I had been craving only twenty-four short hours prior. Yet there I was, wishing that someone I barely knew had invited me to lunch. *We would have hit it off. I know it. I know it without a doubt,* I think.

So then why? Why was it that I always found myself alone?

There I was, in an absolutely stunning location and throwing myself a pity party. Silently, I decided to kick it off with a toast to myself. In an attempt to *not* make it a pity party, I consciously decided to announce to my inner self that I was in a position of strength. That I actually loved my own company. I was enough. But before I was able to applaud my own toast, I unexpectedly swung to the opposite side of the pendulum. I fought with my inner dialog. *What was so wrong with me that I was perpetually alone? That guys that I was interested in never seemed to have real interest in me? Why, why, and why?*

I dove into the depths of those desperate thoughts for the better part of the afternoon.

Eventually, I managed to pick up my phone and FaceTime with my sister. I couldn't help but complain to her about how pathetic I was. She did what a twin sister does best—virtually smack me upside the head with a dose of reality.

"Look around you!" she said. "Look at those palm trees and the beautiful sun on the horizon. Listen for a moment . . . what do you hear? The sound of the ocean. Take a moment and tell me three things about what you see that you truly appreciate and are grateful for seeing right now."

Like a good sister, I listened. I knew where this was going and was thankful for having someone in my life who could help bring me out of that depressing pity party. I looked around and told her the three things I was in awe of and immediately felt better.

She went on to point out something so obvious that I hadn't been able to notice while we were chatting. She said, "Look at me. Do you see what's behind me? I'm in a bathroom. That's a toilet. Your nephew is about to come in here and poop and I'm going to have to wipe his butt. Would you rather be here in this bathroom wiping poop off a toddler's butt, or would you rather be enjoying paradise on a solo trip that anyone else would kill to be on right now?"

I laughed. Her dose of reality was much needed and much appreciated. In that moment, I stopped shedding my pity-party tears and remembered why I wanted to be on a solo trip in the first place. And for the record, no, I preferred not to wipe my nephew's butt, which I've been able to avoid for his entire life.

I actually *did* like myself. I didn't need a handsome stranger on a boat to remind me that I was awesome. I already knew this. I didn't need Surf Boy to inundate me with affection and attention so that I felt special. I was able to make myself feel special.

I remembered how I had meditated the evening before and felt great when I woke up that morning. I didn't know that Blue Eyes would be on the boat. I didn't know who would be on the boat tomorrow. All I knew was that my vacation wasn't over yet and anything was possible. As my grandfather used to tell me, "You make your own breaks."

The next morning was my final day of diving. I woke early to watch the sun rise. Cup of coffee in hand and the sound of waves crashing, I felt alive. I thought back to how long I had wanted to visit Costa Rica and that I was living the dream right at that moment. Endless gratitude was running through my veins.

Looking back, I know it would have been fun to spend time with Blue Eyes for the remainder of the trip. Maybe we would have hit it off, or maybe not. Who knows? What I do know, however, is that things don't happen by accident. I am reminded after one morning on a boat with a handsome man, that I will find my person at the right place, at the right time. Until then, I have me. And I am right where I am supposed to be.

# DANCING AROUND POISON IVY

**WHEN HIP-HOP MEETS THE SHENANDOAH MOUNTAINS.**

"Goddamn it," I muttered under my breath. There wasn't a single handsome *and* seemingly unattached dude in this joint. So much for my sister's input regarding meeting someone.

I was sitting twelve rows back from the altar in a Chicago suburb Catholic church, waiting not-so-patiently for my dear friends to tie the knot.

I had arrived early to scour both sides of the church in search of an impromptu date for the weekend. My optimism about the weekend was quickly fading.

While I scanned the crowd, I caught the eye of Kevin, a friend from Boston. He was one of two people attending the wedding, other than the bride and groom, that I knew. He made his way over and took a seat next to me.

After catching up, I asked him if he had a plus one. He told me he didn't so I asked if he would kindly agree to be my wingman if I was his wingwoman. It was a deal. I had already determined that no one in the church was eligible, so we had our work cut out for us.

The bride was absolutely stunning and the ceremony beautiful. We exited the church and Kevin introduced me to the fellow bachelor party attendees and their dates who were gathered at the church's exit. Since there was going to be a two-hour wait before the reception started, we all decided to head back to the hotel's bar for a drink before catching the chartered bus to the wedding venue.

I decided to go back to my room and freshen up before heading to the bar. Needed to look glowing for whomever may be in attendance. The night was still young, after all.

*DING!*

The elevator door opened. I sashayed into the lobby in three-inch strappy heals, my midi-length angle-hemmed dress in the season's pantone shade of pink clinging to all the right places.

*Oh, hey now.* Who was this handsome fellow checking in at the front desk? He definitely wasn't at the church. He was wearing a suit and looked about the right age to be a wedding guest.

I put on a little bit of a show as I walked past, exhibiting the right mix of eye contact and pretend bashfulness.

He smiled at me! I turned around after I walked by and caught him looking at me.

*Yes.* This guy was most definitely here for the wedding and solo. I was convinced. Thank God the pandemic put a limit on plus ones!

By the time Kevin got down to the lobby, Single Mingle had gone up to his room to drop his luggage.

I very enthusiastically told Kevin that I spotted my target for the evening. He laughed, asking me to point him out later. He'd be sure to help me close the deal.

Hotel bar drinks with the other guests was a blast. I learned quickly that there were three distinct social circles in attendance: the groom's undergrad contingent, the bride's Chicago friends, and their family members. Everyone was friendly and welcoming to the outliers, like me. I knew that this was going to be a great party.

The preparty moved to the picturesque golf club ballroom. The open bar flowed.

Oh, there he is at the bar! Just as I had thought, Single Mingle was here for the wedding.

"The target's in view," I said to Kevin.

Kevin swiveled his head around, followed by his body, to look. He might as well have yelled at the top of his lungs, "Which dude are you checking out, Christie?"

I immediately knew that he was going to blow my cover. "Hey, if you're going to stare at him, there's no way I want you as my wingman. Gotta be cool. This is a covert op."

"Okay, okay," he assured me while turning back to look at me. "I got this. Tell me and I promise I won't be obvious."

After pointing Single Mingle out, Kevin surprised me with a cool surveillance until he locked eyes on the target. Okay, locked and loaded. It was game time.

I knew that I didn't really need a wingman, but a girl will take any help she can get sometimes. Nevertheless, I had full confidence that by the time everyone one was on the dance floor, Single Mingle's destiny would be determined. Give me a few drinks and play some hip-hop, and I'll reel in any fish. I mean that figuratively as well as literally . . . I have no shame doing the fishing pole dance move with any willing partner.

"Christie! Your boy is over there in that group. I'm going to join them," Kevin announced.

"Sounds good. I'm going to play coy. You can work it for me. Let me know what happens."

I wandered around the reception area, chatting up some friendly strangers and getting a fresh drink. Kevin barged back into the ball-room headed straight toward me and was super excited.

"Oh my God, you won't believe it! Your boy is from Northern Virginia too! You guys must be neighbors. What are the chances?"

The groom was originally from Northern Virginia so it wasn't that weird to see a guest or two from the area. It seemed, however, that the universe was aligning for me.

I eagerly asked Kevin, "Okay, so did you tell him that your friend, Christie, that hottie patottie in the pink dress, is also from Virginia and that he should meet me?"

Kevin looked utterly puzzled. "No, why would I do that?"

I was totally confused. "WTF, Kevin! You said you'd be my wingman! That was quite literally the most obvious and natural opening for me! Did you have a couple drinks and forget about our deal?"

He seemed to vaguely remember our conversation in the church. "Oh, yeah, well I'm the wingman for the bride and groom today. Sorry."

I rolled my eyes. "Well, in case you weren't aware, it seems the bride and groom are now married so I'm not sure they need a wingman. Whatever, Kevin. I will close this deal myself. You can watch and learn."

Fast forward through the toasts, salad, and entree. The people at my table were an awesome group. We had a fantastic time during the reception. I announced to my new friends that Kevin, who sat next to me, sucked as a wingman. They laughed and asked which guy I had my eye on. I scanned the tables and pointed Single Mingle out. I announced that I was no longer seeking wing support. I was a solo B52 bomber and this target would go down in due time.

Once the bride and groom had their first dance, Bruno Mars started blaring and everyone over the age of sixty exited the dance floor. It was officially par-tay time!

A dance circle quickly formed, the groom taking center circle. A few people followed into the circle after him. Liquid courage took over and I ventured onto the dance floor and into the circle to show them how New York girls tear it up.

I had felt on fire. As I exited the dance circle Kevin said, "Damn girl. You can dance!"

Before I could respond, the groom tapped me on the shoulder, inviting me into the circle for a dance-off.

Fully feeling the beat, I did a shoulder brush off, some hands in the face, and even my version of hip-hop flossing, in heels no less.

Leaving them wanting more, I exited the circle after twenty seconds or so. I was pretty sure I won, plus I didn't want to give away all my moves in the first song of the night.

The groom followed me out of the circle and said, "Holy cow, Christie! I had no idea you could dance."

Why does everyone always underestimate the coolness of this wide-eyed, petite Italian? "Sorry to smoke you at your own wedding," I said smiling as we hugged it out.

Then—brace yourself—I realized Single Mingle was standing next to the groom. He had come out of the shadows when the music started, just as I had predicted.

The groom said, "Christie, I want to introduce you to my friend, Max. He lives in Virginia too!"

*Damn it*, I should have just asked the groom to be my wingman.

The groom walked off, leaving Max and I to get to know each other. Max said that he had to meet the girl who had just beaten the groom at his own wedding and that I must be a badass, which is exactly his type. I found out that he was into breakdancing and promised to show me some moves.

Hook.

Line.

And sinker.

Max and I had an amazing time. We danced to every type of music that the DJ played. He was a superb dancer. At one point, I was doing God knows what on the dance floor when Max asked me, "Oh, is this interpretive dance time?"

Not missing a beat, I responded, "It sure is," incorporating flipping him the bird into my moves. Later, I found out that he had absolutely loved that and had wanted to kiss me right at that moment.

The party went on and Max eventually kissed me during a slow dance. It was clear he had moves both on and off the dance floor.

The evening ended with a giant after-party, but Max and I decided to throw ourselves our own after-party, with fireworks.

Turned out we both were going to be on the same flight back to DC the next morning, so we decided to grab breakfast together. It was a very nice ending to a wonderful wedding weekend.

Back in Virginia, Max and I continued to see each other. He lived a stone's throw from my sister and meeting up was convenient. I enjoyed his company but was also pretty sure he was not my end all be all. There was nothing wrong with him. Quite the contrary, actually. He was handsome, intelligent, athletic, generous, and full of talented surprises. I just wasn't feeling that it would develop into anything serious.

One weekend, Max invited me to join him and his friends on a boat they had rented for a day. Of course, I said yes, and it was a lot of fun. Thanks to Max, I had the chance to experience a different side of DC and Virginia, from the Potomac River. We docked outside

Georgetown and had a fun-filled afternoon of mulled blueberry vodka cocktails, floating in the water, and dancing to Max's excellent selection of music.

The best part of the day wasn't the water, however. It was Max's friends. I now realized why the universe introduced me to him. I was only three months into my Virginia residency and was making friends. It seemed so easy. I couldn't believe how kind Max and his friends were. They seemed genuine. It warmed my heart.

It led me to reflect back on my five years in Boston. Why had it been so hard for me to make friends there?

After the boat ride, Max invited me to his place for dinner. His condo was clean and mature. Check and check. He also didn't have a roommate. Big check.

He had many interesting collections, among them were his guitars and amps. I asked him if he would play me something, and he agreed. Max serenaded me and it was beautiful.

Feeling the vibe, he invited me to join him on a camping trip for a friend's upcoming and nontraditional birthday party in the mountains. Having enjoyed his company so far, I welcomed this invitation.

On camping day, we drove to a large campsite next to a lake. Before long, a group of more than twenty people arrived, setting up their tents, with countless coolers filled with drinks and food near the campfire. I was able to tell immediately that these were good, fun loving people. I felt welcome and thankful to be there.

A bunch of us decided to go to the lake. So me and my toxic masculinity helped one of the guys carry the giant six-person floaty the quarter mile walk to the waterfront. Max grabbed other floaties and the drinks.

Along the way, I got stung by a bee. One of the girls in the group was very concerned. I announced to everyone in earshot that I wasn't allergic to bees, just sensitive. I needed to head back and pop some Benadryl, or this could go south quickly.

We dropped the floaty at the water's edge and I looked to tell Max that I was heading back so I didn't die. All he said was okay. Strangely, he didn't seem too concerned.

I half expected Max to walk back with me. Isn't that the gentlemanly thing to do when your date's life is in danger, more or less?

Perhaps I had been projecting calmness, which didn't make him think it was a big deal. I don't know. For better or worse, I am not sure anyone has ever told me I project calmness. Regardless, I was on my own to save my own life.

So, by my lonesome, I tip-toed through the grass, back to the campsite, popped a Benadryl and then headed back down to the lake. But where was my date? I scanned the lakeside setup, expecting him to be waiting for me after returning from my near-death experience with a floaty and cold drink in hand.

He was on his own personal floaty a good thirty feet from the shore's edge.

It was okay though. The girl who had been concerned about me asked if all was good. Note to self—she's my ride to the hospital if need be.

I assumed Max, who had been nothing but a considerate gentleman over the past month or two, was just a bit oblivious to my predicament.

The afternoon turned out to be a lot of fun and I didn't die, obviously.

Just like the boat ride a few weeks prior, Max's friends didn't disappoint. If anything, they wildly exceeded my expectations. I had a fantastic time with all of them, eating weird campfire food, and jamming out in lawn chairs in the shallow stream. It was an all-around awesome day.

Before the evening ended, I took a quick, and private, bath in the stream before getting into the three-person tent Max brought.

It's important to recognize that tent size is one of the most misleading things on the planet. A three-person tent is really only big enough for one average-sized human. It's physically impossible to get three adults in a three-person tent if you expect to not be stacked up like lumpy pancakes.

Regardless, Max and I created a cozy setup with our sleeping bags, flashlights, and other gear shoved into the corners to maximize the space.

Getting in and out of a tent is such a pain in the ass. Before tucking in for the night, you should always pee one last time even if you don't think you need to.

Max decided to do exactly that. He unzipped the tent and stepped out, barefoot. I offered him the flashlight since it was pitch-black.

"Nah, I'm good," he said.

"No, really. Can you take the flashlight? There's poison ivy all over the place, you are barefoot, and I told you I'm highly allergic."

"I won't step in it, don't worry." And off he went into the dark of night.

Mind you, I had seen poison ivy in the light of day in about ten different places all around the campsite and had pointed the plants out to him. I made it clear that I needed to be very careful around that vile weed.

Once upon a time, I had learned that while a bee wouldn't kill me, poison ivy might. My second summer at West Point was spent training mostly in the woods, in a place we called Camp Buckner. When you're eighteen or nineteen years old in a co-ed glamping situation, things happen, if you know what I mean. It's called "Buckner Lovin'," and I may or may not have taken part.

While the details are vague in my memory, perhaps because I've tried to block it out, a cute classmate and I decided to sneak off into the woods to make out. We may have passed orientation training but aspiring botanists, we certainly were not.

No, we decided that, out of all the possible places to frolic in nature, we chose a spot that turned out to be a giant patch of poison ivy. Mind you, I didn't know it at the time. In fact, I didn't know it for probably several hours until my entire body started itching.

It itched so bad that I had to see the medic, which turned into a visit to the hospital. We figured out what was going on when my Buckner Lovin' partner also got the itchies. Yeah, one plus one equals making out in poison ivy.

It was so bad that I had to spend several days in the hospital getting pumped with steroids. The oils had gotten into my bloodstream making my entire body inflamed. It was serious enough that my parents made a trip to visit me in the hospital. However, at that time, I pretended to be quite the victim, not knowing how on earth it happened. Mom and Dad, if you are reading this, I'm happy to share, exactly two decades later, what actually happened. Yes, I really know how to make my parents proud.

I spared Max the finer details of my Buckner Lovin' trauma, but was sure to express fifteen times too many that I couldn't risk coming in contact with this horrifying plant.

So, there I was. Sitting in a dark tent waiting for Max to return. Thanks to the pandemic, I had no less than a gallon of hand sanitizer with me.

I watched in the darkness as Max's shadow made its way back to the tent. I was almost certain he had walked barefoot through one of the patches I had identified earlier. But, like any slightly unhinged person, I had a plan.

When Max got to the tent door, I unzipped it like a gate keeper, but I wouldn't let him enter. Instead, I asked him if he could kindly stick out his hands, and I dumped a shit-ton of hand sanitizer on them. "Please rub this all over your legs and feet," I demanded in the sweetest voice I could muster.

To his credit, Max did as instructed. Poor guy, I wasn't done.

I then handed him two baby wipes and asked him to remove the nasty alcohol smell from his legs. Who wanted to cuddle with that stench?

Again, to Max's credit, he did as instructed.

Oh, but wait, I still wasn't done.

"Now, a final blob of hand sanitizer on your hands just for good measure."

Max, yet again, complied. I didn't know who was worse. Me demanding him to rub most of his body down with hand sanitizer or him venturing into the darkness and flirting with my most certain death?

At a minimum, he was a good sport and me only slightly neurotic. Regardless, the rest of the camping adventure was enjoyable.

A week later, Max texted to see if we could meet up that weekend. I told him that I couldn't because I was going hiking with my aunt and uncle. His only response, "Watch out for the poison ivy!"

Touché, Max. Touché.

# THE MAN OF
# MY DREAMS

## WHEN THE MAN OF YOUR DREAMS MAKES
## AN IN-PERSON APPEARANCE.

Suddenly, I was in a dark space. I wasn't here, nor there, nor anywhere. I just existed. I was acutely aware of my own existence. I was also acutely aware that there was someone, or something, directly in front of me.

It wasn't a person, yet it was. The form was white and cloudy, almost as if it was made of tiny white dots that vaguely formed a shape resembling a human. There were no distinguishable features on this cloudy person.

I wasn't scared in the moment. Rather, I was comforted by what I saw and sensed without understanding why.

A thought occurred to me. *This* is what a soul must look like.

As I accepted the nothingness around me, other than this cloudy person that must be a soul, I wondered who this soul must be. Staring at the cloudy face, I could only sense the energy coming from it. It was warm and loving. It was accepting of me. It was here, at that moment, in this blackness, for me and only me.

I consciously decided that this soul must not be a person I had met in my life, otherwise I would have recognized them. Or so I thought.

I was sad. Very sad. I had crawled into bed that night in an extremely depressed state. I had cried myself to sleep over yet another heartbreak from Jake, my two-year Submarine Soulmate. He had done, or not done, something and I had become truly devastated by it. My broken heart, because of him, had become an almost familiar situation. *Why can't I get off this hamster wheel?* I thought. I finally fell asleep, tears dried up and those words ringing in my ears.

Next thing I knew, I was in that black space.

Who was this? It wasn't my Submarine Soulmate, this I knew. Why did this figure have such love for me? The loving energy was palpable. It felt pure as it emanated toward me. I couldn't see the energy but I felt it. I recognized in the moment that this was exactly what I needed to feel.

After standing before me for a moment, the cloudy ball of energy reached up with its cloudy right hand and caressed the left side of my face, starting with my forehead. I immediately felt a surge of loving energy. It was completely and utterly overwhelming in only the greatest of ways.

The cloudy soul moved its hand to my eyebrow, then to my cheeks, my nose, and finally my lips. Slowly, the cloudy soul had caressed my entire face gently and lovingly.

I wondered to myself, *How does it know exactly what I need?*

Then, the cloudy soul turned me toward my right and shoved me off into the blackness.

I looked up and realized that I too was a cloudy ball of energy. A soul, yet conscious and aware of what was happening.

Ahead of me, in the direction that I'd been pushed, was another cloudy soul-like ball of energy. This one was lying on its back as if sleeping. I immediately recognized it to be my Submarine Soulmate from this lifetime.

Leaving the first soul behind, I moved quickly toward my Submarine Soulmate. All I wanted to do was hug him. I wrapped around him, hugging him with a soul to soul hug that only a cloudy ball of energy could do.

And just like that, I awoke to find myself in my bed in the suburbs of Boston. I sat up, tears running down my cheeks, aware of where I was.

*What on earth had just happened? Was that a dream or some sort of reality?*

I had never experienced a dream so vivid, emotional, and realistic. I was struck by the experience and unsure what to make of it. Yet I was comforted somehow by having had the experience. As time went by, I continued to remember the vivid details of what I believed to be some sort of metaphysical experience.

My Submarine Soulmate and I never made a relationship out of whatever our connection was. The love was deep, but clearly not meant for this lifetime.

So, then who had been standing in front of me showering me with love? Why had they pushed me toward my soulmate? Why had I been encouraged to be with him if we were not meant to be? Was the soul I didn't recognize the one I would end up with in this lifetime? Had he been showing me that love is eternal? That I needed to finish the soul journey with my Submarine so that I could continue to grow? And maybe one day he would appear when I was ready? Life continued on and I had none of the answers.

Several years went by and I thought about the experience often. I relived it over and over when in need of feeling love. In my deepest and darkest lonely moments, I recalled the loving caresses and energy as if experiencing them for the first time. The dream had been so vivid that I was able to, while fully conscious, feel the experience again. Years later, remembering the dream still brought tears to my eyes because I knew that love was out there.

During my dating adventures, I had on occasion met a few strong connections that had made me stop and wonder if they were that soul of my dreams, but the energy just didn't seem to fit with anyone.

I decided that the soul from my dream may not be "The One" for this lifetime. Maybe they were just a soul to help me get through a tough time. Nevertheless, for comfort, I continued to draw upon the memory in times of need.

Two and a half years from the night of the dream pass by and I was sitting on the floor in front of a fire. Next to me was a pizza box and what was left of a large pie. I was holding a glass of malbec in my hand.

A handsome man was sitting on the floor too. He was looking at me with a soft smile on his face. I was rambling on about God knows what and he just continued to listen patiently and calmly. It was almost like he couldn't keep his eyes off me despite the nonsense coming out of my mouth.

Then, this handsome man reached up with his right hand and touched my forehead. He gently caressed my face as I continued to ramble on, not really paying attention to what he was doing. Eventually, I stopped talking so I could take in what was happening. It felt so wonderful. It was as if he saw me at that moment like no one had ever seen me. While he caressed my face in the exact way I had experienced some years before in the dream, and repeated over and over in my head since, in that moment I wasn't thinking about the dream. I was living in the moment.

When he finished touching my face, I couldn't help but reach out to him. As I began to caress his face, gently touching is forehead and eyebrow, he closed his eyes then flinched, as if what I was doing was not welcome.

He was startled. Why was he flinching? I asked him what was wrong.

He said that what I was doing was very intimate, but it was okay, I could continue. In the moment I thought it odd. Hadn't he just done this to me?

I continued to caress his face the exact way he had mine. I took it all in, appreciating all the features of who he was. It felt incredibly natural, like the most natural thing in the world having this unbelievably intimate moment with someone I had only started to get to know.

Two days later, I suddenly remembered my dream. It occurred to me that exactly what had happened in my dream had happened in real life. I asked myself if he was the soulmate of my dreams, just as I had wondered about others I had dated. The resounding answer was yes. I felt certain that he was the soul from my dream some years prior.

You would think that this was where I got my happy ending. "An almost forty-year-old spinster struggles to regain her life back after a long-term relationship goes up in smoke followed by several years of dead-end dating. Then, literally the man of her dreams appears before her, and they live happily ever after."

Sadly, that was not how the story went for me.

After that night in front of the fire, he and I had a few more intimate moments where we both confirmed that there was a connection between us. I learned that on the day we had met, he had laid eyes on me first. He said it was as if he had blinders on, seeing no one else but me in that exact moment. When I turned around, I felt instantly drawn to him. I knew within fifteen seconds that this was someone I wanted to get to know. And with time, the more I believed him to be the most amazing man I had ever met.

Despite the affirmation of an initial spark, a relationship never developed between us.

I know that I was ready for that connection, but looking back, he wasn't. The timing was not right. I had a history of giving more than I received in relationships, and I needed to protect myself from yet another heartbreak. Eventually, during this relatively short period of getting to know each other, we pushed each other away.

Some time went by before I reached out to him. I shared my thoughts and feelings with him because I didn't want to live with regrets about not sharing how I felt. I even told him about the dream that I had several years before and that I believed it to be him. I asked him if he was ready for something with me, but he wasn't. He promised me that when he was ready, I'd be the first person he calls. For whatever reason, I believed him.

In the meantime, I decided I needed to live my life. Even though I was convinced that he was the soul in my dream, I recognized that perhaps we weren't meant to be together in this lifetime. All I could do is all that I should, which was live my life to its fullest.

That was exactly what I did as hard as it was at times. It is what fills the pages of this book. I got back out there and put my best foot forward in dating. I went on a ton of dates. I consciously went into every date with an open mind and heart. As the weeks turned into months, I took up new hobbies like learning to golf and scuba dive. I focused on my mental health with deep introspection and healing through therapy and meditation. I took care of my physical health and increased running to seventy miles per week, a threshold I never had thought possible before. I continued to learn about myself and who I was, what I needed, and where I wanted to go in my life. I took care of important things in my life that I had put on the back burner, which helped me feel like my life was being propelled forward. I decided to change my job and pursue a step up in my career for professional growth. I then decided to finally leave Boston and find greater happiness in my personal life by moving to Virginia. I was on an upward trajectory and felt empowered, healthy inside and out, and confident about what my future held.

Of course, I still often thought of my soulmate. How could I not? We were connected. I decided that when he crossed my mind, I would do for him what he did for me in my dream so many years before. Rather than be angry at the situation, I turned my emotions into gratitude for having had the experience. I imagined touching his face with kindness and love and then turning him to the side. Then I imagined giving him a push in the direction he needed to go so that he could continue his life's journey of growth. I thanked him for being a part of my journey and wished him nothing but happiness. Then, I very consciously turned my attention inward. It wasn't easy, but I had no choice. Finding gratitude and peace from the whole situation was the fuel for my future.

After a year of not seeing one another, we found ourselves face to face.

It was a platonic meetup, but it was obvious that a connection was still there. I felt it. I saw how he looked at me, almost reading his mind. There were a few moments where the energy between us was palpable. He felt it too. I knew this too.

So then why the resistance? Why didn't he run toward it? Wasn't this what he wanted too?

During that interaction I remained cool, calm, and collected because I was determined to not make the same mistakes of my past. I couldn't convince someone to be with me. They must want it. I needed to once and for all let go of my control issues. I knew what I wanted, but that didn't mean someone else knew what they wanted, what they were willing to go for, or if they even wanted me.

I was so proud of myself and the growth I had made. I had been focused on myself and living my best life. But I also couldn't stop thinking about him, more so in this moment than ever. Seeing him reminded me of how I had felt some time before. Or perhaps my feelings had never left even though I had been out there living the fullest life I could. I couldn't be sure.

As if the universe was testing my growth, he and I came face to face yet again only a few weeks later. He told me that he had just recently, since I had seen him last, started to date someone that he believed to be his soulmate. I was confused. Wasn't the spark between us still there just a couple of weeks ago? Had I imagined it? Didn't he promise me that I would be the one he would call when he was finally ready to date?

He expressed that he was very comfortable around me but didn't have any romantic feelings for me. He was in love with this woman and she with him. He had never felt a connection like the one he felt with her. I asked him so many questions, but he didn't have any real answers. It didn't make sense.

I told him that the connection and feelings he described about this other woman was how I felt about him. I put it all out there. I was devastated. *How could this be?*

When he said that she was a lot like me, I told him that didn't make me feel better. In fact, it made me feel worse. I didn't understand. I was confused, taken aback, and so sad.

But, for some reason, I also felt a bit of relief mixed in the deep sadness. Maybe this was the universe telling me to finally let him go. I had clearly not released all my control issues. I had no choice but to accept what he told me even if it didn't make sense.

Before we said goodbye, I asked him if I could do for him what he did for me in my dream. He knew exactly what I was referring to and said yes. I don't know why he agreed. It was an intimate thing to do and he was supposedly madly in love with another woman. Yet I knew that we were soulmates too.

I reached up and I touched his face one last time. I caressed one side before cupping his face in one hand and started to caress the other side of his face with my other hand. He closed his eyes yet reached out and held me. He pulled me in for a hug and I put my hand on his heart, as if I was sending him positive love and energy straight to his soul center. We stood there hugging. It was heartbreaking. I didn't want to say goodbye but I had to. I told him that he was a very special person and deserved greatness and happiness. He told me the same.

And just like that, he was gone.

# THE ONE

STARRING IN MY OWN SAPPY, ROMANTIC MOVIE.

L ike most middle-aged spinsters out there, I enjoy a relaxing evening on my couch with some unnecessary carbs while watching a mind-numbing, unrealistic, and sappy movie. *It helps turn the brain off after using it all day,* I tell myself.

However, at some point during the movie I always wonder if there is such great demand for movies like this because of spinsters like me who have nothing better to do on a Friday night. Or perhaps spinsters and non-spinsters alike enjoy a nice fairy-tale plot that doesn't require brain power, allowing them to have it play in the background while making holiday cookies?

I ultimately always ask myself, *Do I watch these movies to make myself feel better or to make myself feel worse?* I can't be sure.

The story line, without doubt, varies very little from one movie to the next. It usually goes something like this. . .

A big city girl with a high-powered and successful career finds herself in an unknown town in West Virginia. Her boss has insisted that she leave the comfort of her high-rise and the bustling city to take care of some business out in the boondocks.

On the winding country road, just a few miles from her intended destination, she picks up the speed of her top-down, red convertible, her long hair perfectly blowing in the wind.

*POP!* A loud noise accompanied by a giant cloud of dust emerges from the back of the car and remnants of a tire fly off into the distance. Her expensive convertible swerves wildly, but she regains control as dust flies everywhere. She pulls off the dirt road so she can assess the situation. She gets out of the car slowly, one beautiful long leg at a time, designer pumps and all.

Having never been on a dirt road in her life, as she walks toward the blown tire, the big city girl steps on a piece of gravel in just the precise way that causes her to teeter ever so slightly. She may be beautiful, but an athlete she is not. Her ankle buckles under her and she lets out a gasp, as only the most delicate of women can do. She stumbles and ultimately falls to the ground. Oh no, her dress is now covered in dirt! Her knee is bleeding, her hair disheveled. She quickly finds herself exasperated by the situation. Tears begin to fall from her eyes.

Why did her workaholic boss send her to the middle of nowhere for this stupid job assignment? Why hadn't these country folk fixed their roads? How hard was it to get pavement out here? Where was she anyway?

She pulls her phone out of her designer purse and, after an exaggerated minute of holding it up toward the clouds, finally realizes that she has no cell service. *What oh what is a city girl to do?*

*Oh my, is that the sound of an approaching car?* She looks up to see a green pickup truck tumbling down the road. As it gets closer, she notices it has a rusted front bumper and a big dog sitting in the passenger seat. The truck slows.

The sight of the pickup disgusted Big City Girl. She hated the country already and she had only just gotten there.

Behind the wheel is a handsome man. He pulls the truck over, manually rolls down the window, and looks over toward her. He has beautiful eyes, a scruffy face, and a full set of teeth. A micro-expression flashes over Big City Girl's face as she takes note of how handsome he is, but it quickly changes to disgust and frustration from being dirty. No matter how handsome this man may be, Big City Girl wants nothing to do with any of this.

In an ever so slight southern drawl he asks her if she needs help, which she obviously does. Being the rude city girl that she is, she snaps at him and comments about how unacceptable it is to be stuck on dusty roads in a godforsaken town with no cell reception. No cell reception! How uncivilized!

He laughs and shakes his head. *Just another big city girl,* he thinks. Since he's a kind and generous human being, he knows that this self-absorbed, rude woman needs help, plus it could be several hours before another car comes by.

He offers her a ride to the local car shop saying that maybe they could tow her car and fix it. Having no other choice, she grabs her purse and oversized suitcase from the tiny trunk of her convertible, puts her sunglasses on her resting bitch face, and reluctantly struggles to step up into the rusty pickup in those ridiculous heels. She pushes the big drooling dog away from her, further annoyed by the friendliness of an innocent pet.

Meanwhile, the audience is drooling at the man in the driver's seat. He has a ringless left hand, sense of humor, good looks, and personality to go with it. How is he still single, we all wonder as we pause from taking a bite of our frozen pizza, eyes glued to the TV screen. Presumably, because his hometown has a population no larger than four hundred people and his high school sweetheart broke his heart a decade ago, leaving him in a perpetual state of vulnerability and singledom. Or maybe he's just waiting to meet the right lady. Damn it, this female character is destined to be his match by some fluke of the universe! *Ugh*, we think, as we resume eating our pizza.

Let's fast forward through the next eighty minutes of this mind-numbing television movie. As it turns out, Big City Girl is stranded in the middle of nowhere for weeks while her car gets fixed, but she's able to nevertheless complete her work assignment, which coincidentally has everything to do with the hot country man. Coincidences are abundant in this movie.

Hot Country Man never stops being an incredibly patient gentleman despite the rudeness of Big City Girl. However, bit by bit, he chisels away at that chip on her shoulder. By the middle of the movie, she stops wearing four inch heels and inappropriate dresses, replacing them with outfits suitable for country living. By the end of the movie, he falls madly in love with her, and she falls madly in love with him.

After twenty-one days, her work assignment done, Big City Girl is miraculously no longer the same person. She decides to quit her high-powered job and the great salary that goes with it. No more city life for her! Instead, she'd rather live in the middle of nowhere with Hot Country Man raising goats and making jam.

That, my friends, is pretty much how every pathetic story line goes in the sappiest of all sappy romantic movies. It is easy to get sucked into them. Don't we all want to fall in love during a fall harvest dance in a barn filled with flannel and pumpkins? Yes, I believe it's every girl's dream. But the cost is quite high, I've noticed.

Independent, successful, ambitious women are inevitably painted as rude, self-absorbed, and high maintenance, incapable of picking a decent man until she's literally hit over the head with a pumpkin. And, without fail, the extremely hot starring male figure sees in her what literally no one else can. Slowly, he brings out in her everything that we wish she had shown up with in the first place, such as decency, kindness, generosity, intelligence, and security. How is it that he can change her just by his existence in less than ninety minutes?

Well, the answer to that is simple. It's television, and piss poor television at that. However, I still watch it and I bet you do too.

As a successful, independent, and ambitious woman, I reject the cliché characterization of the modern career woman. I also reject the underlying premise that the success of her career plays a large part in her ongoing singledom. Disregard for a moment the fact that this television character is often rude, insecure, and oblivious, as that's besides my point here. I want to know why she must change who she is to find her soulmate? Can't the success in her professional life compliment success in her love life? Or are these mutually exclusive circumstances that are exacerbated as she approaches the desperate spinster age?

I think it just makes good television. And by good, I mean not "good," but you get what I'm saying.

Many of us are conditioned to believe that there are acceptable and predictable life paths that are driven by societal expectations: education, career, love, marriage, kids, the suburbs. Preferably in that order too. Should this all happen by a reasonable age . . . say, thirty-five for a woman? Beyond that, you're approaching the expiration date. Something must be wrong with you to not have hit those milestones, right?

On the contrary, what about a thirty-five-year-old man who has a strong career and is going places? Well now, he's obviously a ripe avocado waiting to pick up a damsel in distress on the side of the road. Like a fine wine, he just gets better with age.

For a long time, I have rejected society's expectations and milestones pertaining to life choices. Maybe my life didn't go the way it "should have" because of a self-fulfilling prophecy, or perhaps it was my rejection of these societal "norms." I don't know which came first, but I do know that how I choose to view myself cannot and should not be defined by someone else.

Why must someone else see in me what I should be able to see in myself? I don't need to be in a relationship to feel the fulfillment of love.

I accept those things about me that change. Every day, I work to improve myself and what I can offer this world. I accept that gratitude is the most powerful emotion, even when a situation seems dire or out of control. I choose to believe that I alone can create my own destiny, but that can only happen when I know who I am and when I believe that I am worthy.

Over these past five years, I have grown and changed in so many ways. I picked myself up off the floor after my ten-year relationship ended. I wiped my own tears with each broken heart I suffered. I held my own hand through my cancer diagnosis and treatment. I moved a few times and made bold career changes. Yes, I had people in my life that loved and supported me through these times, but I was still very much alone every step of the way.

These difficult experiences taught me that even though I was single when they happened, there was one person who had always been there without fail. That person was me.

Mind you, I didn't like myself at times. I didn't appreciate myself at times. I didn't, dare I say it, love myself at times. Even worse, at times I didn't even pay attention to myself, letting other things and people take priority in *my* life.

How was I so oblivious to the love that was right in front of me, waiting for me to see and accept it with open arms?

Thankfully, I eventually found it and learned to appreciate that love through therapy, a dedicated practice of meditation, and daily doses of positive affirmations. It didn't happen quickly, but when I actually listened to my inner self, I recognized that I needed to change my own narrative if I ever wanted to change my future.

And guess what? I started to change from the inside out. I began to recognize the deep-seated, unhealthy fear and pain within me. They were like a toxic security blanket that needed to be thrown out with the trash. Yet I was strangely attached to this blanket despite its dirtiness, almost finding comfort in the familiarity of its stench.

It took a lot of time and work, but eventually I was able to let go of that security blanket and replace it with a nice, clean quilt, which was made up of the various patterns and intricacies that make me a unique human being. It has been immensely freeing to look back and see how far I have come in my own self-discovery and development.

From what once began as a blog that attempted to turn depressing dating stories into ones riddled with humor and levity, this book was born. I found writing the blog cathartic and satisfying. As a bonus, my single and nonsingle friends alike seemed to enjoy my stories and encouraged me to write more. I found their support to be both reassuring and accepting of me and my journey.

I wrote this book for myself, first and foremost. By putting ink to paper, I share with the world, unapologetically, who I am. This book is nothing more than a proud exclamation for the love I have for the most important person I will ever have in my life—me.

I am not perfect, nor will I ever be, but my goal in this journey of life is to be the best person I can be. I believe that my own self-love will create an opening in the universe that will allow the right person and opportunities to enter at the right times. I have full confidence that I will attain all that I desire one day, wherever I may be, and regardless of whether I swipe right on a dating app ever again.

Not if—but when—I meet "The One," I will have nothing but gratitude for being able to share my life with another beautiful soul. It is from this place I will find love, kindness, and patience to traverse through the hardships and joys of life. I know this because I have already found these things deep within myself while on my own journey. With the right person, the power of love harnessed from a place of gratitude can only bring greater love and gratitude.

Along my journey, the biggest revelation I have had is that I don't need to find love to be happy. I am happy because I love myself. It is that simple. Sometimes self-love falters when life gets particularly hard, but I am proud to have developed the ability to recognize the warning signs and rein them in. For that, I am so proud of myself.

One day while meditating a thought came to me, which I have clung to in only the most positive ways. It is mentioned early in this book, and it is repeated as the last line for a reason. I am eternally grateful for having found myself on this journey, through both the good times and the bad, ultimately finding the self-compassion to truly accept and love myself. I wish the same for you.

**THE LOVE WE ALL SO DESPERATELY SEEK IS ALREADY WITHIN US.**

# ABOUT THE AUTHOR

By day, a marketer in the biotech industry. By night, a dating blogger with a super-secret audience. Christiana Cioffi found blogging to be a creative and cathartic process throughout her long and winding journey in search of love. From there was born *An Unapologetic Spinster*. Prior to her biotech career, Christiana served as a captain in the US Army for five years, including two years deployed in support of Operation Iraqi Freedom. She holds a BS in management from the United States Military Academy at West Point and an MBA from the Kelley School of Business at Indiana University. Her professional awards and recognitions include a Bronze Star, a Combat Action Badge, and a Medical Marketing and Media (MM+M) Award. She is a breast cancer survivor, an avid runner, and a scuba diving enthusiast. Christiana resides in West Virginia with her geriatric cat, Ellie, and her rescue German Shepherd mix, Frankie.

@UNAPOLOGETIC_SPINSTER
WWW.LINKEDIN.COM/IN/CHRISTIANACIOFFI
WWW.UNAPOLOGETICSPINSTER.COM